# GOD IS NOT ENOUGH,
# HE'S TOO MUCH!

*by*

*Jesse Duplantis*

**Harrison House**
Tulsa, Oklahoma

*God Is Not Enough — He's Too Much!*
ISBN 1-57794-020-2
Copyright © 1997 by Jesse Duplantis
P. O. Box 20149
New Orleans, Louisiana 70141

Published by Harrison House, Inc.
P. O. Box 35035
Tulsa, Oklahoma 74153

# Contents

**Harrison House** • P.O. Box 35035
Tulsa, Oklahoma 74153

In Canada books are available from:
Word Alive • P.O.. Box 670
Niverville, Manitoba • CANADA ROA 1EO

*For this cause*

For this cause I Paul, the prisoner of Jesus Christ for you Gentiles, if ye have heard of the dispensation of the grace of God which is given me to you-ward: how that by revelation he made known unto me the mystery; (as I wrote afore in few words, whereby, when ye read, ye may understand my knowledge in the mystery of Christ) which in other ages was not made known unto the sons of men, as it is now revealed unto his holy apostles and prophets by the Spirit; that the Gentiles should be fellowheirs, and of the same body, and partakers of his promise in Christ by the gospel: whereof I was made a minister, according to the gift of the grace of God given unto me by the effectual working of his power.

Unto me, who am less than the least of all saints, is this grace given, that I should preach among the Gentiles the unsearchable riches of Christ; and to make all men see what is the fellowship of the mystery, which from the beginning of the world hath been hid in God, who created all things by Jesus Christ: to the intent that now unto the principalities and powers in heavenly places might be known by the church the manifold wisdom of God, according to the eternal purpose which he purposed in Christ Jesus our Lord: in whom we have boldness and access with confidence by the faith of him.

*Wherefore I desire that ye faint not at my tribulations for you, which is your glory. For this cause I bow my knees unto the Father of our Lord Jesus Christ, of whom the whole family in heaven and earth is named, that he would grant you, according to the riches of his glory, to be strengthened with might by his Spirit in the inner man; that Christ may dwell in your hearts by faith; that ye, being rooted and grounded in love, may be able to comprehend with all saints what is the breadth, and length, and depth, and height; and to know the love of Christ, which passeth knowledge, that ye might be filled with all the fulness of God.*

*Now unto him that is able to do exceeding abundantly above all that we ask or think, according to the power that worketh in us, unto him be glory in the church by Christ Jesus throughout all ages, world without end. Amen.*

*Ephesians 3:1-21*

# Chapter One
## God Is Not Enough —
## He's Too Much!

Let's say you have a kid, and tomorrow morning, bright and early, he comes into the kitchen. He takes out his favorite cereal bowl. It's a big one with painted cartoon characters on the side. He gets out a box of cereal and begins shaking some into his favorite bowl. He's smiling and cheerfully humming as he shakes out the flakes. You're cleaning up a little and, just when you stop what you're doing to get the milk for your son, you feel a tug at your pants. "Hey, Ma! Can I pour the milk in the bowl today? Can I, Ma? Huh? Can I? Huh, huh? Can I?"

You smile and say, "Yeah, son. Go ahead, get the milk out of the fridge and put some in your bowl." The kid smiles and happily trots towards the fridge. He takes the jug of milk out and, clutching it to his chest, he slowly tilts it down and begins to pour the milk into his bowl. He's wobbling just a little from the weight of the jug, but he's got a pretty good hold. And soon enough, you see him start to pour a steady stream of milk into his bowl. He giggles a little as the milk starts to coat the cereal. You turn around to finish what you were doing.

Meanwhile, the white stuff is still pouring. And it's coming a little close to the rim. The flakes are starting to float. The raisins are starting to gasp for air. There go the nuts. They're doing the back-stroke just trying to stay afloat! But the kid doesn't think anything of it. He hoists the milk jug on his shoulder and continues grinning as the stream of milk turns into a thick, creamy waterfall.

That's just about the time you spin around and see the first wave of milk splash over the rim of the bowl. You freak out. "Stop, stop, stop! You're pouring too much! It's going to...!" But you're too late. The law of gravity beats you to the punch and there it goes, over the edge of the bowl, onto the kitchen table and onto the floor.

Then he does something you can't believe. Instead of letting up on the flow, he lets out a squeal of delight as he turns the wobbling jug upside down! Now it's gushing, slapping into the bowl and running over onto the table! Milk is everywhere! Splashing on the table, splattering back up on your kid. It's coating the legs of the table and running across the floor. Big pools of white are everywhere! And the kid is still squealing and giggling as he tilts the jug back a little and lets up on the flow.

You are furious. Anger is boiling within you. Hot with fury, you clench your teeth, widen your eyes and hiss, "What's the *matter* with you, boy? Do you know how much money that milk costs?!!!"

You see, to you that's waste. But to God? *It's prosperity.* To the world what that boy did was rebellious. On top of that, he was just plain wasteful. But to God, he wasn't either of those things. He was experiencing what it meant to have a cup that *runneth over!* God is *more than enough.* David knew it. Over and over he sang verses that openly praised God for His vast goodness. But he didn't just sing about it. He experienced it. I love it when I read David's words. **My cup runneth over** (Psalm 23:5)! **Yet have I not seen the righteous forsaken, nor his seed begging bread** (Psalm 37:25)!

Religion through the ages has acted like the prudent parent who always says, "Stop, stop, stop! That's wasteful! You don't need that much!" They're in the guilt business. They're in the restraining business. They're in the business of telling you what you *can't* have.

But God isn't. He's in the business of telling you what you *can* have. And He isn't afraid to make a few people angry by filling your fridge with milk. He's got enough in there to fulfill all your needs and much, much more. Don't you think it's time you got yourself a jug and started pouring? Why keep all of His goodness, mercy, health, prosperity and peace sitting on the shelf?

Get your favorite bowl out, child of God. It's time to experience *all* of God's goodness. It's time to experience *The God of Too Much.*

## Paul's Revelation of The God of Too Much

Paul the apostle was a great man of faith who had a divine revelation of God. I believe that few have really understood the Lord's nature as well as Paul. In fact, the entire third chapter of Ephesians is a testament to Paul's belief in The God of Too Much.

In this letter, Paul openly shows us how amazed he is by God's abundant grace, glory, riches, power and love. In fact, his language goes bankrupt just trying to get it all down on paper. Why? Because Paul recognized that God was too much! All that God is and all that God does just can't be verbalized in human language. And Paul knew it.

Are you ready to find out about The God of Too Much? Great. Then get out your Bible and turn to chapter three of Ephesians, Paul's letter to the church at Ephesus. I've written the Scriptures here in the book, but I'd like you to read your Bible as well so that you can see it for yourself!

Let's read it together. Let's try to grasp the emotions Paul felt as he wrote this amazing letter. I want you to recognize the tone of excitement Paul writes with as he shares his revelation of God with the church at Ephesus. As we read through the chapter, I paraphrase a little as I feel led. Let's start with verse one.

**For this cause I Paul, the prisoner of Jesus Christ for you Gentiles, if ye have heard of the dispensation of the grace of God which is given me to you-ward** (Ephesians 3:1-2). Paul is one loyal guy. He shows us this when he refers to himself as a voluntary prisoner of Jesus Christ for the Gentiles. Paul's life and actions were Jesus', and his purpose was spreading the news about the distribution of God's grace to the Gentiles.

Basically he's saying that those of us who weren't under the Old Covenant — which was strictly for the Jews — now had the opportunity to partake of God's grace!

**How that by revelation he made known unto me the mystery; (as I wrote afore in few words, whereby, when ye read, ye may understand my knowledge in the mystery of Christ) which in other ages was not made known unto the sons of men, as it is now revealed unto his holy apostles and prophets by the Spirit** (Ephesians 3:3-5). I love verse four where it says **...when ye read, ye may understand...** because it shows how powerful reading the Word is. It unlocks the mysteries of Christ, which is Jesus' anointing! It wasn't revealed before, but through Jesus it now is. Here Paul starts telling us about how much God is and how much God does.

**That the Gentiles should be fellowheirs, and of the same body, and partakers of his promise in Christ by the gospel** (Ephesians 3:6). Yeah! Because of Jesus' blood, we can have the promises of God that were once only for the Jews. Everything God said they can have, we can have too. It's ours through Jesus!

**Whereof I was made a minister, according to the gift of the grace of God given unto me by the effectual working of his power unto me, who am less than the least of all saints, is this grace given, that I should preach among the Gentiles the unsearchable riches of Christ** (Ephesians 3:7-8). There Paul goes again! He's talking about grace! He's telling us how excited he is that God's grace has been given to him, the last one who should deserve it. He's telling us that God gave Him grace so that he would be able to preach about the unsearchable riches of Christ! *Unsearchable* means you can't find the end. The riches of Christ go on and on and on!

**And to make all men see what is the fellowship of the mystery, which from the beginning of the world hath been hid in God, who created all things by Jesus Christ: to the intent that now unto the principalities and powers in heavenly places might be known by the church the manifold wisdom of God** (Ephesians 3:9-10). Ooooooh! I love it! What was once a mystery hidden in God from the beginning of the world is now available for all mankind to see! The manifold wisdom of God is available to the church (which is us — we're the church). And now, even the powers of the air know that we have the wisdom of God!

**According to the eternal purpose which he purposed in Christ Jesus our Lord: in whom we have boldness and access with confidence by the faith of him. Wherefore I desire that ye faint not at my tribulations for you, which is your glory** (Ephesians 3:11-13). In other words, we don't have to be afraid to approach the Father. We can be confident knowing we can come to the Father on *His faith*. Whose faith? *His* faith! Then Paul tells them, "Don't be sad about my tribulation for you! It is your glory! It should show you we're making the Devil scared!"

See, the Devil is no match for God. And he can't give you something you can't handle through Jesus! God doesn't send tribulation to teach you something. The Devil just tries to stop God's plan for your life by sending tribulation. (Did you get that? Read those last two sentences again. I want you to know that like you know the back of your hand!)

The Devil tried to stop Paul and he'll try to stop you. But don't worry about it. Think of it like Paul did: it's your glory! You're intimidating that idiot and he's trying to shut you down. But **greater is he that is in you, than he that is in the world** (1 John 4:4)! You will be victorious!

Now the rest of the chapter is where Paul really starts trying to get it all on the page! Notice how he humbly bows down before Jesus and begins praising Him right in the middle of his letter to the Ephesians! Then he begins to jump from one subject to another in an attempt to squeeze his revelation of who God is into words.

Notice the tone in which he writes. **For this cause I bow my knees unto the Father of our Lord Jesus Christ, of whom the whole family in heaven and earth is named, that He would grant you, according to the riches of His glory, to be strengthened with might by his Spirit in the inner man** (Ephesians 3:14-16). Might is the ability to do what God said by His Spirit ruling our hearts. Paul is on his knees in reverence to God asking that He give strength to the Ephesians and now to us! Where does that strength come from? The inexhaustible riches of God's glory! And how are we going to get it? Through the Spirit who lives within our inner man! Who is that Spirit? The Holy Spirit, who dwells in every born-again believer through the acceptance of Jesus' redemptive blood! Man, I love this! It's preaching me so happy, I think I just might buy another copy of this book!

**That Christ may dwell in your hearts by faith; that ye, being rooted and grounded in love, may be able to comprehend with all saints what is the breadth, and length, and depth, and height** (Ephesians 3:17-18). Here Paul begins by explaining that Christ, the Anointed and His Anointing, dwells in our hearts by faith. Then he tells us that our faith will only work if we're rooted and grounded in love! By the time he starts trying to explain God's love, he runs out of adjectives! That's when Paul grabs his spiritual measuring tape and starts talking about depth, width and height, praying to God that we'll be able to comprehend it!

And I don't know about you, but I'm praying I can comprehend it, too! Just thinking about the breadth, depth and height of God's love is mind boggling! There aren't enough words in any language to describe God's love! Why? Because God *is* love. Just think about that for a minute! God and His love are one thing. *God is love!* This is some heavy stuff!

So you can't separate God from His love and you don't have enough words or emotions to describe it. His love is bigger than you can grasp with the natural mind. He is more than you need and more than you can handle. *He's too much!*

**And to know the love of Christ, which passeth knowledge, that ye might be filled with all the fulness of God** (Ephesians 3:19). Now, he's telling us that God's love passes up our knowledge! His love is beyond our brain! We can't fully know it in our mind and so Paul's having a hard time describing it. His language is becoming bankrupt on him!

And because we can't grasp God's love with our intellect, Paul tells us that we must be **filled with all the fulness of God** so that we may **know the love of Christ.** And finally, when he can find no more words to describe the fullness of God, Ephesians 3 ends with Paul encouraging the Ephesians (and us) to use the power that we have in Jesus to move the hand of God.

**Now unto him that is able to do exceeding abundantly above all that we ask or think, according to the power that worketh in us, unto him be glory in the church by Christ Jesus throughout all ages, world without end. Amen** (Ephesians 3:20-21). Whew! After all that, I don't know about you, but all I can say is "Amen," too!

What I want you to notice about this passage is Paul's exasperation. Do you notice how he keeps stretching this whole thing out? Do you notice how he keeps adding more and more adjectives together in what seems like an attempt to describe God?

I love how he starts out with God is **able**. And then he adds, God is *able to do*. Then, he continues to add more! God is **able to do** *exceeding.* God is **able to do exceeding** *abundantly*. God is **able to do exceeding abundantly** *above*. God is **able to do exceeding abundantly above** *all*. God is **able to do exceeding abundantly above all** *that we ask*. God is **able to do exceeding abundantly above all that we ask** *or think*. And then he gives the requirement: God is **able to do exceeding abundantly above all that we ask or think,** *according to the power that worketh in us!*

Can you feel Paul's exasperation as he tries to get it all in? The man practically throws his pencil down and says, "What else can I say about You, God? Is there anything else I have words for?"

## Jesus Knew His Dad Was Just Too Much!

I love to read how Jesus set up Philip in John 6. Jesus had been preaching up a storm and everybody was so enthralled by him, the crowd followed him over the Sea of Galilee. Jesus was up on the mountain sitting around with His disciples when they came over. A multitude of them started walking towards Jesus on the mountain. Knowing that they'd traveled to hear Him, Jesus looked at Philip and said, "Where can we buy some bread around here, so the people can eat?" But the Scripture says that Jesus deliberately asked Philip, just to test him, because He already knew what He would do.

So Philip, in so many words, says, "Man, Lord, we can't feed all these people! Do you see how many of them are out here on the grass? We just finished a meeting, Jesus. But even if we took the money from the offering it wouldn't be enough to feed all of these people! Shoot, if we could, they'd only get a bite!"

Jesus just looked at him. Andrew, who was Simon Peter's brother, must have felt sorry for Philip, so he searched around to see if somebody hanging around had a little food. Then he said, "Look, I found this kid who's got a two-piece fish dinner. But there's no way it'll be enough for all these people!" He was probably thinking, "What am I going to do, disobey the Son of God? He's asking for something to eat. At least I've got something. At least a few will get a bite to eat today." But Jesus says, "Make them sit down on the grass."

So the disciples get everybody in order...all five thousand of them. Jesus took the two-piece fish dinner, blessed it and then gave to His disciples so that they could feed the people. Philip and the rest of them began tearing up the fish and bread.

Of course, you know the story. That's when the miracle happened. As they would give one person some fish and bread, what little they had left would multiply! And before you knew it, everybody ate and was satisfied. Nobody was hungry — and when it was all said and done — there were twelve baskets of leftovers!

It's not like they needed the leftovers. Everybody had eaten enough, and there wasn't a fridge to keep the fish fresh anyway. Makes you think, *Hmmmm, maybe God miscalculated when He started multiplying the fish and loaves*. No! No! No! God didn't make a mistake! He over-provided because it's just His nature to do that! He's The God of Too Much. He's not just enough. He's more than enough!

So, how does it go again? **Now unto him that is *able*! Now unto him that is able to *do*! Now unto him that is able to do *exceeding*! Now unto him that is able to do exceeding *abundantly*! Now unto him that is able to do exceeding abundantly *above*! Now unto him that is able to do exceeding abundantly above *all*! Now unto him that is able to do exceeding abundantly above all that we *ask*! Now unto him that is able to do exceeding abundantly above all we ask or *think*! Now unto him that is able to do exceeding abundantly above all we ask or think *according to the power that worketh in us*!**

Yeah, I know it's a mouthful. But don't knock it, because it's a mouthful of prosperity! When you break the Scripture up, each added word becomes a promise of what God can and will do! It really helps to get hold of what Paul was trying to tell us about God's nature.

# Chapter Two
## How Did God Get Such a Bad Rap?

Sometimes I feel sorry for God. I really do. I mean, think about it. Here is the Creator of the universe, the Maker of everything, and He just can't seem to get His creation to think good things about Him! Everywhere you go, people are always blaming Him for something.

It seems like God has gotten a bad rap for centuries. Throughout time, He has been lied about, labeled and criticized. He's been blamed for everything from catastrophes and sickness to death and poverty. Rarely do we hear anything good about God.

Why do you think that is? Is it because God really does cause destruction, disease and poverty? Or do you think that perhaps the people who say He's doing these things really don't know Him at all? As you might have guessed, I'm of the opinion that those who bad-mouth God don't know Him at all. They may know *about* God, but they don't *know* God.

Knowing God and knowing *about* God are two totally different things. You can know *about* God simply by being raised in a Christian home or reading a couple of chapters from your Bible each night. You can know even more by going to church every time the doors swing open or enrolling in a good Bible college. These things will guarantee that you know *about* God. But they won't guarantee that you'll really ever *know* God. And that is what you need to do if you want to see any manifestation of His power in your life.

Knowing God doesn't just mean being "saved," which is the modern-day Protestant church's terminology that means you've accepted God's redemptive plan and have accepted His Son, Jesus, as your personal Savior and Lord.

If you are to really know God you must spend time with Him, and not just in mindless lip service, but in real communication. If a real relationship is ever going to form, communication has got to be two things: frequent and fluent.

And that is where most people who think badly of God go wrong. They might pray frequently, but it's rare that they have conversation that could be called fluent.

In fact, over my twenty years of ministry I've found that people who have a bad opinion of God usually don't have that fluent communication with God. Sure, they're good people. And they're praying good prayers. But the reason why they don't succeed in having what God's Word says they can have is this: they don't have real, biblical hope...and because of that, they aren't able to exercise faith.

Now, I know that is strong. And I promise you that I am not cutting "good people" down. But, hope is critical. Hope is "earnest expectation" that God can and will do what He said.

It comes before faith. It paves the way for faith. It's the preparation for faith. Without it, faith can't emerge. And faith is what makes things happen!

> **Now faith is the substance of things**
> **hoped for, the evidence of things not seen**
>
> (Hebrews 11:1).

Faith is so critical because it works things out in the supernatural realm so that the answer to your prayer can come to fruition in the natural realm. In essence, faith moves God's hand on your behalf. Nothing pleases Him more than when His creation believes Him.

Frequent and fluent communication with God will help you to know God. So if you're thinking that God is too majestic and powerful to talk to "little old me," you're stifling your own ability to hear God's voice.

Many people do this and end up never really knowing their Father God intimately. I mean, how can you really know somebody if you don't communicate well with them? How can you know God if you don't give Him the opportunity to speak to you? How do you do that? Well, by believing that He will! That's faith! Sometimes even if your mind says something different, you've just got to believe.

Get into your Bible and study. Find out what God has to say about prayer, about communicating with Him. It'll be enough to blow your mind! Prayer is a whole other book entirely!

If you don't find out what the Bible says about communication with God, if you don't search to *know* God, then you'll only have your own ideas *about* God to go on. And you want to go deeper than that. In chapter 4, I'll talk more about prayer...about knowing God.

## Hand-Me-Down Lies

Sadly, most people's ideas about God come from years of passed-down religious lies. Sickness. Poverty. Hard times. They were all sent from God to teach people how to be holy. These kinds of hand-me-down lies spread like wildfire. Taught that they weren't good enough to really know God, generations settled for knowing about God.

Many were condemned instead of encouraged. Taught to expect nothing from God, most people lived in fear of God.

They blamed Him for everything bad and thanked Him for everything good. Consequently, generations of people with good hearts and good intentions slowly grew blind to The God of Too Much.

I'm certain that if people really knew God, if they really had a good relationship with God, they would never think of blaming Him for every unexplained bad thing that happens in life. They'd believe the Bible instead of the traditional hand-me-down lies and would study to know the Truth.

## Who Could Stand It but God?

Isn't it easy to see how I could feel sorry for God? Don't you? Is there anybody else you know who has gotten such a bad rap for so many years? Who else but God has had generations upon generations of families spreading vicious, untrue rumors about Him? Who else but God could be patient enough not to come tearing off the throne and start throwing lightning bolts? Who else but God could stand it? That in itself should show you the merciful nature of the Father!

Shoot, if it was me I'd jerk the slack out of everybody continuing to talk bad about me! I'd catch them while they're sleeping and holler in their ears!

"I ain't like that! Why don't you read my book?!" I wouldn't let them continue another day blindly walking in ignorance...perishing for lack of knowledge. But God is not that way. He isn't rude, and He won't push Himself on anybody. He'd rather be patient. He'd rather let His mercy and grace tell the tale. He'd rather let them go on forever.

These days it has become so normal to think badly of God that many don't even give a thought to doing otherwise. Either through ignorance of the Word, misinterpretation of Scripture, or religious tradition, many people still think that it is more holy to be poor than to be rich, more holy to be sick than healthy.

But nothing could be more untrue! Nothing could be more disappointing to a good Father than to be thought of as an angry and spiteful tyrant by His children.

## So Who Started the Rumors?

So who started all this bad talking about God? Who gave everybody the crazy idea that God is out to give us sickness and poverty to teach us something? Well, think about who started the first rumor on earth.

You know who it was. The Devil! Satan started the first rumor by lying to Eve about God's plan. I can just hear the Devil saying, "Go ahead and take a bite, Eve. You won't die! God just doesn't want you to eat it because if you do, you'll know as much as He does." There you have it, rumor numero uno: *God is a liar and He wants to deceive you to keep you under His thumb*.

Did God ever give Adam and Eve the impression that He was like that? No! Never! God set them in the most lush and beautiful garden on the whole earth. He let Adam name everything alive and then visited the both of them just about every afternoon. He was not only their Father, He was their best friend! Does that sound like a scheming, poverty-loving, sickness-embracing god to you? Does that sound like a cruel, evil god to you? Of course not! It sounds more like a loving and generous God who likes seeing His children enjoy His creation.

The Devil started a rumor about God. Eve bought the lie and bit the fruit. She gave the fruit to her husband. He ate and they both died spiritually that day. Until Jesus shed His precious blood, everybody born inherited their spiritual death. But God had a plan! His only Son, Jesus, came to earth and died on the cross a sinless and blameless man. As the supreme sacrifice for the sins of the world, Jesus' redemptive and life-giving blood enabled every person on earth to be washed clean in God's sight! Once we receive (or accept) Jesus as our personal Savior and Lord, we can come back into right standing with God! We can once again experience what God originally intended! Except now, there is a twist.

## The Twist

The twist is that we're not in the garden anymore. We're still living in a world run by Satan until we die or Jesus comes back, whichever comes first. We live in this world as lights in a dark place (Ephesians 5:8). Because that is what the world still is: a dark place.

There are still people who haven't heard the Good News. There are still people searching for the answers to life that can only be found through Jesus. If there weren't, we'd just die and go to heaven right after accepting Jesus because there would be no use for us here on the earth. But there is a use, a purpose, for us and it is the most important of all. What is it? Spreading the Good News about God and His plan of redemption through Jesus! Letting people know that God is good and His mercy endureth forever!

But how can we spread the Good News if we're not sure that God is even good? How can we bring in the light if we're barely shining?

It's time to put the lies and rumors of Satan to rest...to lay aside tradition and find out the truth...to stop pointing the finger at one another and start pointing our finger to the originator of all lies. And who might that be? Go ahead, say it out loud: the Devil! What a creep.

## Why Would Satan Even Care?

The Devil and his demons continue to be the sole rumor-starters about God on this earth. They lie about everything to anybody who will listen. But over many centuries they've learned to be cunning about it, and disguise many of their lies.

They've gone so far as to even get some of their lies in the church. Satan has gotten people believing all kinds of negative trash about God so that he can keep them down in the dumps all the days of their lives. He's got preachers teaching that God sends sickness.

Why? So that you won't believe God for your healing, and consequently will live defeated, which is a slap in the face to Jesus who died on the cross to take on sickness!

Remember, Satan doesn't really care about you. I hate to break it to you but, on your own, you aren't that important to him. In fact, he probably wouldn't even mess with you if you weren't God's creation. See, it's God he hates. And it's God who he's trying desperately to get back at.

So, what will he do about it? He'll try to destroy God's people — that's you and me — by tying our hands in this life, to make the Gospel message ineffective to the rest of the world who might be won to God otherwise. And what would be the best way for the Devil to do that? Get into the church system. Get church folks to do his dirty work.

One of the biggest lies Satan spreads is about prosperity. He's been working on that one forever. Why do you think it's such a hot topic among Christians?

He's been trying to nip prosperity in the bud for centuries. Why? Well, if you look to the Bible you'll find out why. Deuteronomy 8:18 says, **But thou shalt remember the LORD thy God: for it is he that giveth thee power to get wealth, that he may establish his covenant which he sware unto thy fathers, as it is this day.**

Establishing God's covenant (getting the Gospel message out) is an expensive venture. Why is it so expensive? Because we were also given the command in Mark 16:15 to **Go ye into all the world, and preach the gospel to every creature**. Going into all the world takes bucks!

So, what do you think is the first thing the Devil is going to do about those Christians who take Deuteronomy 8:18 and Mark 16:15 seriously? He's going to try to stop them! He'll try to stop you from succeeding financially so that you can't establish God's covenant within the earth. Because the Devil knows that if you could, you would! Makes sense, doesn't it?

Better yet, that Devil had a plan to make poverty religious! Can you believe it? He actually sold the lie that it's holy *not to* have and prideful *to* have! What a load of bunk!

I bet the Devil got all the demons together and had a meeting about it. They probably all chimed in saying, "Man, Satan, you are one smart devil! What a great concept! Let's get everybody to believe that God doesn't want anybody to have anything. That way the Gospel won't spread, and we can hang out even longer on the earth! What a great idea! Anybody who wants to burn any sooner than they have to, speak up. Nobody? Great! Let's make it happen!"

It is almost comical when you hear it put that way, isn't it? But truth is truth: the Devil is a con artist. And he is trying to con you out of every blessing Jesus has died to give you. One of them is prosperity, both spiritual and financial. In fact, that idiot has your money right now. Yeah, that's right. According to Proverbs 13:22, **the wealth of the sinner is laid up for the just**. So he has your money. He's spending it right now. And that's not funny!

## When Poverty Became Holy

I grew up in a poor Cajun family. My Mama and Dad loved God and we were at the church every time the doors flew open. Much of the rebellion against God that I went through was a direct result of the hypocrisy I noticed in church life. People always talked about how great God was, but I didn't see much greatness. They always talked about how God healed, but we were always sick. They talked about giving, but we never received much in return. Even as a small boy, I knew there was something wrong with the picture.

I can remember firsthand what poverty felt like. Down in the bayous of south Louisiana, I can remember my Mama driving us up to the old Royal Castle hamburger place. They sold these little, tiny burgers that were maybe two inches square. But they had ketchup and onion pieces on them. And they always had the softest bread. Besides that, they were only sixteen cents each. We loved them.

We were so poor, if we'd seen a Burger King Whopper, my brother and I would have surely thought we made the Rapture! We didn't know what a Whopper was. A Big Mac attack? Let me tell you, a burger to us was either a two-inch Royal Castle or a slice of bread folded in half with a fried piece of meat slid over it for flavor. No, you couldn't have the whole piece of meat. You might get a little to crumble up. Your best bet was to slide some of the grease left in the pan around on your bread so that you could get the taste of meat. I'm not lying. It was that bad.

Anyway, my Mama and Daddy would drive up to the place and, even though the tiny burgers were only sixteen cents, my Mama wouldn't order anything for herself. She couldn't eat because we couldn't afford to buy everybody a Royal Castle hamburger. So she bought me and my brother one each. I remember that.

Now, she thought I never noticed that she didn't eat because we couldn't afford it. She probably thought I was too young to notice. I couldn't have been more than six. But she always did say that I was a thinker. She would just say she didn't want anything. But I knew better. Everybody liked Royal Castle burgers. My Mom especially.

I always heard Mama talking about how wonderful God was. So, when I'd see my Mama sit there with us and not be able to eat a little hamburger I would think to myself, *why doesn't God feed my Mama?* Now, I was thinking with a six-year-old mind.

I always saved a bite of my hamburger for my Mom. It was so little. Two bites and it was gone. But, even if I wanted it — and I always did — I'd say, "Ma, I had enough." And she'd say, "No, boy. You need to eat that."

"No, Ma. I don't want it."

Then I'd go home and when I'd get to my room I'd close the door and cry. One time, I couldn't stand it anymore and even though I knew she might get mad I finally asked her what I wanted to know. "Why don't God help us, Mama?"

She said, "Well, you know, you've just got to stand and believe. You've got to love the Lord, Jesse. I mean, things are just hard sometimes."

"I don't want that kind of God!" I said.

"Don't you say that! Jesse, don't you ever say anything like that. I'll slap you silly if you say that again, boy!" she'd say.

"Okay, Ma. I won't say it no more." And I wouldn't. But I thought it. Oh, I thought about it a lot. And I never wanted to go to church because even as a little kid I didn't believe God was wonderful. I couldn't see Him doing anything for my family.

What happened? Religion. That's what happened. It crushed my family with its poverty teaching. They could have taught us how to rise above, how to shake off the poverty mentality and use the principles of God to experience blessing. They could have encouraged us to use faith to bring those blessings about. But they didn't.

We were already poor people. We didn't need any help to get poorer. Religion just strengthened the poverty mentality. It made it worse because poverty wasn't looked down upon, it became holy. It meant that you gave everything to God and you weren't concerned about earthly things. After religion stepped in, you couldn't shake poverty off my family if you tried. They clung to it because it was all they knew.

## Poverty May Look Good to the Religious World, but It Stinks in the Nostrils of God

Have you ever wondered why religion picked up on poverty? Is there anywhere in the Bible where God says that He wants His people to live in poverty? Go ahead, look it up in the Word. There is nothing in there about God thinking poverty is holy. In fact, Ephesians practically screams out God's goodness and abundance!

Some religions actually ask their leaders to take a vow of poverty in an effort to make them more holy and acceptable to the Lord. This "poverty-is-holy" mentality is nowhere in the Bible. It is a man-made doctrine that stinks in the nostrils of God.

As a kid, I had enough sense to know that poverty wasn't good. I heard about heaven and it sounded real nice. Meanwhile, we were poor. And I hated being poor. I hated that other people looked at me and knew I came from a poor family. It was embarrassing to wear the same old clothes all the time. At least we were clean and fed, though. My Mama washed every day and she could cook great. But being poor was degrading. And I decided at a young age that I wouldn't stay poor. I had talents. I knew it. My Dad taught me a few chords on the guitar and by the time I was five years old, he was using me to play music for the church. I was the only musician around. I would play guitar at our church and my Dad would loan me out to the church down the street, too.

I played hymns by ear. Of course, we were too poor to send me to music lessons, so I never learned how to read music, although I always wanted to. But I could play anything you put in my hand. And my talents drew me out of the church and into the world for one simple reason: money. People would pay money to be entertained. And I was willing to entertain them as long as they liked.

By the time I was a teenager, I was making good money. I'd work a regular job after school until about eleven at night, then I'd go home, sneak out and play music in the bars and clubs until the early hours of the morning. I'd come home, sleep a couple hours and wake up to go to school. It was hard, but I didn't care. I was making money. I was having fun. And

I was wearing clothes that were new and, on top of that, I thought they were pretty cool.

I won't go into many details of my testimony, but I will tell you this. I married my wife, Cathy, and we left southern Louisiana. Within just a few years I was playing rock music with a band, touring and making $13,000 a week. Back in the seventies that was some serious dough. I think it's a lot for today! But I was drinking a fifth of whiskey a day and doing all kinds of drugs.

Cathy got saved during this time and she was always asking me to go to church with her. So one time I agreed. I told her, "Look. I'm going to go, but just so it will get you off my back. One time, that's it." She was thrilled. She invited my brother and we all went together.

We walked through the back doors of the church and everybody turned around and stared. I'd forgotten how I looked compared to church people. I had long, wavy, choco-late-brown hair, cut in a shag. Do you remember that seven-ties cut, the shag? They say it's back, but I don't know. I think it should remain history. Anyway, I was skinny and dressed like a musician from the early seventies drug culture. These church people's eyes were as big as quarters.

We sat in the back. They started singing an old, familiar song: "Bringing in the sheaves...bringing in the sheaves...we will come rejoicing, bringing in the sheeeeeaves." Sheaves? I didn't know what a sheave was when I was kid and I sure didn't know then! I looked around and I noticed something. Everybody in the church was fat. This one woman had the fattest ankles I'd ever seen. Hunks of flesh literally draped over her shoes. I wasn't looking at them critically really, I was just noticing it. Then it dawned on me. All these people could do was eat. That's it. Everything else was a sin. The old days of religion as a kid came to my mind.

So, I was sitting in the back and listening. The preacher said his thing and then at the end he asked everybody to bow their heads. I bowed mine.

And, you know, here I was in church...a sinner. I was a man who needed Jesus. A man who had a lot of money, who could pay off a church. A man who could bless kids and send them on church trips or whatever. A man who really had a soft heart. And because I never respected money, because I knew I could always make it, I was a man who didn't mind giving.

My head was bowed and then I heard a voice bellowing from the front of the church.

"Hey, you! You back there with the long hair! Do you want to get saved?"

It dawned on me. He was talking to me! And I heard Cathy start speaking in tongues. She knew me. She knew that I wouldn't let anybody try and harass me. I looked at Cathy and loudly said, "What? What's the matter with this idiot?" And Cathy just kept praying.

"What's the matter with this fool?!" I hollered. Then I started cussing. And I mean I started cussing. Right there in the church and I didn't care if they all heard it. I wanted them to.

I stood up and said, "I'll tell you one thing, you blankety-blank-blank-blank! I'll kick your blankety-blank-blank from here to blankety-blank!" (I'm sure you can imagine how I filled in those blanks!) My brother grabbed me and said, "Whoa, Jesse. No, don't hit him!" I was on my way. Preacher or no preacher, I wanted to knock that guy between the eyes. He was so fat, I could have hit his head against the wall then watched it bounce back sixteen times!

Man, he saw that I was mad. My brother grabbed me by one arm and my wife grabbed me by the other and they started to move out of the pew. But just as they had me through the back doors, I turned around.

"Hey, look. I apologize. I guess I shouldn't be cursing in church."

The preacher just stood there. The deacons didn't say anything. Nobody said anything.

"Look, I want to give something," I said as I pulled a big wad of bills out my jacket. I always kept a couple of grand on me back then, just in case I wanted to buy something. I had a stack of hundred-dollar bills and I was peeling them off one by one. I peeled about $800 off and I began to walk toward the front with my offering. The preacher reached out to take the money and I put it in his hand.

"Won't you put this in your church," I said. "Maybe it can help you out. I didn't mean to get too mad, you understand?"

He nodded and said, "Oh, I appreciate that. Thank you." I turned to walk off and went, "Oh, wait a minute. Wait. Wait. Wait!" And I pulled my money out again. And when I did, the preacher smiled. He opened his hand to receive another offering. When he did I reached out, grabbed my money and pulled it right out of his hand.

"If I'm not good enough for you, neither is my money!"

I took the money, folded it back into the thick wad I had in my jacket, turned around and walked out.

I told Cathy, "I will never darken the doors of a church again. That's it. Never." I asked her, "Cathy, how come my money is good enough, but I'm not?"

Cathy was so sweet. Her eyes welled up and all she said was, "The Lord loves you, Jesse. The Lord loves you." And she hugged me.

But I did not darken the doors of a church for years after that episode.

Until one night when I was getting dressed in a hotel for a gig. I was in Boston, Massachusetts, when I flipped on the tube and saw Billy Graham. And I watched him talk. I felt like saying, "See my hair? I'm a sinner. Smell this breath. I'm an alcoholic. See my nose? It's filled with white powder. Cocaine. See my chest? It's drugs that are pumping my heart so fast, I've got purple splotches. I'm a sinner."

But Billy Graham didn't condemn me. He didn't ask for my money. He asked me for my life. He let me see the real Jesus. He showed me love like Paul said...**love which passeth knowledge** (Ephesians 3:19). And that night I reached out to that love. I couldn't do it in front of Cathy, so I got up off the bed and went to the bathroom. That was the night I accepted Jesus into my life. And I've never been the same since.

What I always liked about Billy Graham's ministry is this: he never condemned me. He never talked about "long-haired hippie freaks." He actually seemed to care for my soul. He showed me a side of God that I'd never seen, even as a child growing up in church.

You see, I should have never left God. But it was poverty of thought that made people think so small...to not expect anything from God. But God never said that. Since I've gone from *knowing about Him* to *knowing Him*, I know that He never wanted that to happen at all. If you read His Word you'll find out that He loves His people. Many have just been led astray by lies.

God told us that He was **able to do exceeding, abundantly above all that we ask or think, according to the power that worketh in us.** Don't you think it's time we start believing Him?

## God Never Intended for His Kids to Live Without

God never intended for His kids to live without. He sent Jesus so that we could have life **and have it more abundantly** (John 10:10)! Jesus died so that we might enjoy life with each other and partake of all that this life has to offer that is good. Every good and perfect thing comes from above (James 1:17, author's paraphrase.)

Poverty is not good. It was not originally in God's plan for man. He didn't create poverty as a blessing to Adam and Eve. He didn't create trees in the Garden of Eden that gave no fruit! He didn't create soil that refused to make vegetables grow! God never would have given Adam the ability to feel hunger if He did not intend to fulfill him with physical sustenance.

Poverty is a curse that came about when sin entered the earth after the fall of mankind. Suddenly man had to work by the sweat of his brow and still receive very little from the land. Sin did this, not God. Man, not God, gave the earth over to Satan by inviting sin in. Sin warped the way things were supposed to be. Poverty entered the earth.

But do you know what? Even in the Old Testament, before Jesus came and redeemed us from that curse that sin brought, God prospered those who lived pure and holy lives before Him. Throughout the Old Testament, you find that those who walked after God eventually had favor and became prosperous people in the earth. Go through the Old Testament and you'll find out that almost every major player who tried to live a pure and holy life before God eventually experienced blessing.

Do you think that was a coincidence? No! That's God! He is the one who empowered a man to prosper back then just as He empowers men to prosper today.

> Psalm 35:27 (NKJV) says, **Let them shout for joy and be glad, Who favor my righteous cause; And let them say continually, "Let the LORD be magnified, Who has pleasure in the prosperity of His servant."**

What about a few others? Scriptures like these tell us what part God has in the prosperity of His children:

> **The blessing of the LORD brings wealth, and he adds no trouble to it.**
>
> **Proverbs 10:22, NIV**

> **When God gives any man wealth and possessions, and enables him to enjoy them, to accept his lot and be happy in his work — this is a gift of God.**
>
> **Ecclesiastes 5:19, NIV**

> **...No good thing will he withhold from them that walk uprightly.**
>
> **Psalm 84:11**

You shall remember the LORD your God, for it is He who gives you power to get wealth....

Deuteronomy 8:18, NKJV

The LORD shall open unto thee his good treasure...and...bless all the work of thine hand.

Deuteronomy 28:12

A faithful man shall abound with blessings....

Proverbs 28:20

Misfortune pursues the sinner, but prosperity is the reward of the righteous.

Proverbs 13:21, NIV

Those who seek me diligently will find me. Riches and honor are with me, Enduring riches and righteousness. That I may cause those who love me to inherit wealth, That I may fill their treasuries.

Proverbs 8:17-18,21, NKJV

The Lord is my shepherd; I shall not want.

Psalm 23:1

"For I know the plans I have for you," declares the Lord, "plans to prosper you and not to harm you, plans to give you hope and a future."

Jeremiah 29:11, NIV

These Scriptures prove to you that God is not enough. He's too much! He blessed His kids even before Jesus came to town to save the world. And if He did it back then (before Jesus), how much more do you think He'll do now that you're redeemed? It gets you  thinking, doesn't it?

God ain't sitting up there on a golden throne looking down His nose at His creation, seeing poverty as holy and blessing us with sickness! Whoever thought that one up was listening to lies.

Poverty isn't God's brain-child. It came from the Devil. It's a curse and it's bad news. The Good News is  Jesus! His blood redeems us from every curse.

## You're the Church!

In the world, money is power. And for centuries it hasn't been too much different in the church. By preaching poverty, they kept the people poor and the church rich. But God never intended for it to be that way. He intended for both the church *and* the people to prosper! After all, who is the church? You are! I am! *We are the church!* Together we are the body of Christ, united  in our faith, united in our love for Jesus! The church isn't some building down the road! It is you. And you are entitled to all the prosperity that Jesus lived and died to give you.

You are entitled to a rich and rewarding relationship with Jesus (spiritual prosperity), a healthy body and mind (physical prosperity), and resources vast enough to bless your family and all the other families of the earth (financial prosperity). Sound like a tall order? It is! Jesus did a great thing at Calvary! He made the Way for each of us to experience the goodness of God in every facet of our lives.

Sadly, prosperity has become something of a curse word in many Christian circles today. But I believe that even the Christians who once frowned upon prosperity will come to see the truth of prosperity.

Sure, we know that there have been some folks who took the prosperity message and abused it for their own gain. This was wrong and we all know it. But the obsessions of a few misguided Christians do not discount the message. God is not an evil Father. He's good. He's love! And His heart's desire is to be close to His children, to bless them with health and prosperity in this life and in the life to come.

As His heirs we aren't supposed to be poverty stricken and down in the dumps! We're to be totally fulfilled spiritually, physically and financially!


## Any Time There's Money, There Are Crooks

For some people, prosperity might as well be a four-letter word. The sound of it makes many people's eyes bug out like they just heard their Mama cuss.

But God doesn't think prosperity is a cuss word. His whole joint up there spells out luxury. Sure, there are people who cheat, steal and lie. Some of them are in the church. They're wolves in sheep's clothing, trying to make a buck off God's people.

But don't get all excited over it. Can you think of one place in life where there are no crooks? Hey, there are crooks everywhere. Every field has them. There are crooked doctors, but not all doctors are crooks. There are crooked businessmen, but not all businessmen are crooks.

Anywhere there's money, there are crooks. The church has money, so the church is going to have a few crooks. Don't let it shock you. That's the world. That's what sin does to a place.

But just because there are a few crooks, don't discount the entire thing! I hate to use this cliché, but you wouldn't throw the baby out with the bath water, would you? You wouldn't neglect The God of Too Much just because some crook took advantage of His goodness, would you?


## At Least Try to Live What You Preach!

What blows me away is how many preachers sneer at the prosperity message but still take up an offering on Sunday morning. I think that's hysterically funny. I mean, if you don't believe in having anything, then go broke! Hey, don't get mad at me. At least I'm living what I'm preaching. I preach prosperity and I'm prosperous. I figure, if you preach poverty then why are you even trying to live decently? Why not starve to death and really give God the glory! Drop dead. Go out with a bang!

If you're a preacher and you're against prosperity then why don't you tell the people what you *really* believe next time you take up the offering. Say something like, "Now some of you who are going to give in this offering will be blessed. Some of you...well, you're gonna go broke because you know how God is. Sometimes He does, sometimes He don't."

No way! You never hear anybody say that. Preachers who don't believe in prosperity really just don't believe *the people* should prosper. The church, well, that's different, they say. That's a load. There isn't any difference at all! If the church believes it should prosper, then it should also believe that the people should prosper. What's fair is fair.

Hey, money is power. We all know that. And they don't want you in the power seat. Why? Because they want to be in control. It's easier to rule poverty-stricken people because, let's face it, they're happy to get anything.

Now, I know this is serious. And I know I'm knocking over a few golden cows here. But it just isn't right! I'm so tired of people thinking that serving God means being poor! I'm so tired of hearing the church condemn prosperity while their walls are lined in expensive stained glass and gold! The church is the people! And serving God means being rich in every facet of life! Poverty isn't for God's people! It isn't even for the birds! God provides for them, too, you know (Matthew 6:26.)

## Finish This Sentence:

### Jesus Said, In My Father's House There Are Many...
### a) Mansions  b) Trailers

I've been to heaven. I know some people don't believe it, but I really don't care. It happened. God sent an angel and that angel escorted me there in 1988. I was there five hours and fifteen minutes, and did you know that in all that time I never saw a poor person? I never saw a homeless individual or anyone who was despondent or depressed. I never saw sadness. I saw no hiding. And everyone — and I mean everyone — got along. That in itself was amazing.

I saw praise. I saw worship...worship like I've r
earth. It made me fall on my face. I heard laug
filled my ears with sounds I've never heard on e

I'm an advocate of biblical prosperity. But you know I really could have cared less about the gold streets, even though I'd heard so much about them. And, yes, the sight of them was spectacular. All of heaven was breathtakingly spectacular. But what I was more interested in was the people occupying the place.

And let me tell you something — I didn't see one despondent, beat-down, depressed and complaining person. Not one! I didn't see one person griping, "I tell you what, things are tough, man. Gabriel broke his wing last week. We got trouble up here. God had to cut back. It's bad, Jack! He had to go to hell and get some money and bring it back to us." No, I didn't see any of that! People were prosperous there. They were full of joy! They were full of laughter! And they didn't seem bothered or aggravated about the fact that gold paved the streets and jewels held up the city. They were *all* prosperous.

If you have a hard time with extravagance, I must let you in on a secret: heaven is extravagant. God is extravagant! You can't get around the fact that the place is extravagant. I think that if reporters from the major television networks went to heaven, they'd pass out. They couldn't get a spiteful story on the news fast enough! But you know for all that beauty and all that wealth, I didn't once hear God say, "Hey, boys. Check out the sheen on my gold street. Check out that monster pearl on the gate outside!" No, He didn't brag about it. But if you look in the Bible, you'll find out that He made no point of hiding it either.

Even Jesus talked about material things in John 14:2 when He said, **In my Father's house there are many mansions. If it were not so, I would have told you.** He didn't say, "In My Father's house there are many trailers." He said *mansions*, nice places!

Now, why do you think God's building mansions for His children? Why is he having a nice place built for you? Well, um, let's see. Could it possibly be that, uh, maybe...He loves you? Yes!!! *He loves you!*

He loves you so much that He's planning a place for you that will go far beyond what you can ask or think! And if He loves you enough to plan a home in heaven for you, don't you think He loves you enough to get you a decent place here on the earth?

# Chapter Three
## The True Nature of God

The true nature of God is totally different from the character-assassinating rumors Satan has been spreading about God since the beginning of time. God is good and if you don't believe it, just ask Him! Look around in His Word and you'll see that *God is not enough. He's too much!*

His grace is too much! His mercy is too much! His love is too much! Everything He *is* and everything He *gives* is just too much for us to use up! The God of Too Much is especially "too much" when it comes to His kids. The "G" in God might as well stand for generous, because according to the Scriptures that is what He is.

He never gives you an offering unless he stomps on it a little bit to get more blessing into your bucket. Luke 6:38 tells us He presseth it down, He shaketh it together and it runneth over! He's squeezing more in there than you can handle! He's not into just getting by, He's into abundance!

## God's Not Looking to Keep You Down; He's Looking to Raise You Up!

God isn't looking for a way to keep you down! He wants you to be successful! He's not looking to keep you homeless, hungry, in need of clothing or a car. He wishes that you be **...perfect and entire, wanting nothing** (James 1:4).

No matter what type of community or society you live in, God wants to bless you with more than enough to meet your need. He wants you to be successful in everything you set your hand to do.

If you live in a village and you need healthy animals to be successful, then God wants to provide you with more of the healthiest sheep and cows than you have land to raise them on! If you live on a bean farm and you need a strong and plentiful harvest of beans each year, then God wants to provide you with more beans than you know what to do with! Whether you live in the suburbs, the city, a village or on a farm, God wants to supply you with more than enough! Why? So that you'll have enough not only for your own household, but so that you'll have enough to give to others in need and spread the Good News of Jesus to the ends of the earth!

> **And you shall remember the LORD your God, for it is He who gives you power to get wealth, that He may establish His covenant which He swore to your fathers, as it is this day.**
>
> **Deuteronomy 8:18, NKJV**

## God Even Takes Care of the Little Things

Don't you just love to see the faces of your family and friends when you surprise them with a gift? How about when you do something for them that they weren't expecting? I think we get that love of surprises from our Father, God. He just loves to go out of His way for us! Sometimes subtle and sometimes not, God's surprises always seem to remind us of His thoughtful, generous and caring nature.

As you may know, I am a traveling minister and I'm on the road preaching the Gospel more than I'm home. When you live according to a calendar like I do, sometimes time can speed away from you. But God always seems to take care of me.

A few years ago, I found myself traveling and realized that it was just a couple of days before my twenty-third wedding anniversary. I have been married since 1970. (And just in case you're wondering, it's been to the same woman. I have to say that these days!)

Up to that point, Cathy and I'd had eighteen years of bliss and five years of hell! Oh, yeah, complete hell! Those first five years were terrible! But it wasn't her fault. It was mine. I was a heathen dog from hell with hair down my back, alcohol breath you could smell for a mile and pride that would make a rooster look humble. It was a good thing that Jesus came into my life when He did because if He hadn't who knows what would have happened to my marriage. We'd either be divorced or I'd be dead today! Thank God that Jesus made me realize what a good thing a wife is.

Anyway, Cathy and I were traveling on the road together almost twenty-three years to the day since we said "I do." And I realized after a few attempts en route to the next meeting that this woman just wasn't going to leave my side! I tried to ditch her a few times so that I could arrange something nice for our anniversary, but she just wouldn't go away! So consequently I ended up empty-handed the day before our anniversary. No gift, no flowers, nothing. Nothing but my Cathy, that is.

It was the day before and we were on a plane flying to the next meeting. (Yes, I also forgot about our anniversary when I booked the next meeting. But thanks to Cathy, I haven't done it since!)

So I thought to myself, "I'm going to call that church secretary when I get to the hotel. I'll get her to order me twenty-four long-stem roses for Cathy." I knew we'd been married twenty-three, but I added one to grow on. You know, I wanted to make it nice and I knew Cathy liked flowers.

I was thinking that I'd give them to her from the pulpit at church. To make a long story short, I didn't make it to the phone in time. The church offices were closed. I was disappointed but I thought, "Well, I'll just have to find something special to do on Sunday."

The anniversary came. Cathy and I got ready for church and someone from the church came to pick us up for morning service. Well, wouldn't you know it! All of a sudden, someone came walking up to Cathy and handed her two dozen long-stem roses, just to be a blessing to her! I was so shocked! I told Cathy that I'd meant to do it all weekend long, turned to her and said, "Happy Anniversary, Mama!" I was excited!

I thanked the Lord for surprising me and He replied, "I heard you think it, Jesse." It blessed me so much to know that

God loved me enough to take care of a situation that was as unimportant in the grand scope of things as our wedding anniversary. But He cared for us! And He made sure that He supplied even simple desires! He didn't just give twenty-three roses, one for each year of marriage, He gave twenty-four. Why? Because He's *too much*, and giving just enough wouldn't be abundant.

That is how God is. He is El Shaddai, not El Cheapo! He is just *too much!* God doesn't just meet your need — He goes beyond it into the realm of too much. God is beyond your need, beyond your desire, beyond your want. To just meet a need would be below His standards of abundance. God lives abundantly. And it is His wish that you live and give that way, too.

## Common Questions and Comments About Prosperity

Over the years, I've heard many reactions to the prosperity message. Yet no matter where I go I encounter a couple of common questions and comments about prosperity. Maybe you've wondered about the answers to these questions, too. If you have, I'm glad to share my views on them. I hope they'll help to shed some light on this controversial subject.

## "But Brother Jesse, Doesn't God Only Prosper Us Spiritually?"

This is an issue that has confused so many people. You've got one preacher over here reading a Scripture and proclaiming it as the "proof" that God hates money. And you have another preacher over there reading another Scripture that he says is "proof" that God does *not* hate money! Interpretation! Interpretation! Interpretation!

If you don't really know God...if you don't know His true nature...if you've been taught something contrary to His true nature all your life, you might end up deceived by the lies Satan has started about earthly prosperity. And you just might end up believing some guy who hinges his whole anti-prosperity message on one verse that he's taken out of context and altered to fit his agenda.

That's why you'll find that I've included so many Scriptures in this book. I don't want you to just read Ephesians 3:20. I want you to read dozens of Scriptures about The God of Too Much!

You know, the Bible doesn't say anything about God wanting you to prosper in only one area of your life, even if that area is the most important one. Yes, your spiritual prospering should be first and foremost. In my opinion, prosperity's true definition is the peace of God that passes all understanding. Without peace, prosperity doesn't matter. Without peace, nothing really matters. When you trust in the One Who is backing you, you'll be able to move forward in life without worry. That's peace. Spiritual prosperity is definitely the most important thing because without it you have no real concept about what finances are really for.

With out spiritual prosperity, financial prosperity is just a nice car, nice clothes and a nice house. And what does that mean to anybody else but you and your family? Sure, you look great from the outside. But after you have what you've always wanted, what then?

That self-centered "bless my four and no more" attitude does not come from God. He is a generous God whose love for others outweighs anything else. And if we really know God, His spirit will rub off on us and we'll end up acting the same way! We'll be generous and loving, ready to bless others with our blessing! Now, that's prosperity! (Genesis 12:3.)

## "Why Is *That* Guy Prospering? I Know He Doesn't Know God!"

For people who aren't already prospering in the world, spiritual prosperity will be the key to obtaining earthly prosperity. I've heard many people who get aggravated about their situations. They look down the road at their neighbor and say, "Brother Jesse, that guy down the block is prospering like crazy and I know he doesn't know God!" That's right. You hit it on the nose. The guy doesn't know God. He may not even be saved.

Consequently, he's doing everything in his own strength. And he may be very successful at what he does. He may have learned how to go out into the world and produce wealth. But the rules for you don't apply for him. He's going to hell. You are going to heaven. Big difference. He's working under natural law and, although he is becoming successful at it, there is no peace without Jesus and so it will amount to nothing in the end. He is not prospering spiritually, physically and financially. He only has the financial prosperity, and without the Lord he'll have a hard time making it last for very long.

You, on the other hand, have the ability to work under supernatural law, which is not only more effective in gaining financial prosperity than natural law alone but also helps you to prosper in all the other ways God wants you to!

You see, in this world you may be a good businessman and become wealthy. Many unsaved wealthy people practice godly principles and succeed. Sometimes they don't even know they are God's principles because someone has written a book for financial success that is really just a compilation of godly principles in everyday language! God's principles for wealth will work for anybody who applies them, saved or unsaved.

But once you come to the saving knowledge of Jesus, you have the opportunity to gain *all* that God has for you, spiritually, physically and financially. You *can* work under supernatural law. Jesus paid the price so that you could have it *all!* That guy prospering according to natural law can't get it all no matter how hard he tries. Because without God there is no healing, no peace, no real joy, no true prosperity.

You have the opportunity to experience a full and complete life in God! Prosperity in every area is what God intended! He has plenty and He's ready to pour out a blessing you don't have room enough to contain! Are you in agreement with that? If you are, then you are a candidate for too much! The question is...do you want too much? And if you don't...why?

## "But I Don't Need Much to Be Happy, Brother Jesse"

Chances are, if you find yourself saying this every time somebody talks about prosperity, then you just might not be as selfless as you think you are. Many people who say this kind of thing think they're being humble and content in doing so. I hate to break this to you, but the truth is that you probably don't have God's perspective on prosperity. Now, don't get mad at me! It's His idea, not mine!

I've heard a friend of mine, a very popular minister, repeat a saying that I think sums it all up pretty well. She says, "Poverty won't keep *you* from going to heaven, but it just might keep *someone else* from going to heaven." Now, that is a powerful statement! It shows you that  someone else's life may depend on whether or not you prosper! Lives depend on whether you sow your prosperity into furthering the kingdom of God.

The bottom line is this: financing the kingdom of God takes money. Sending preachers all over the world with the Gospel takes money. Purchasing air time that will enable the Gospel to be televised worldwide takes money. Printing Bibles in different languages takes money. Putting out Christian magazines, books, tapes and videos takes money. Building churches and housing missionaries in foreign countries takes money. Obeying the Scripture's command to **go ye into all the world, and preach the Gospel to every creature** takes money (Mark 16:15)!

Every Christian has been given the responsibility of spreading the Good News throughout this earth. That means that either you go, or you send somebody who is called by God to go.

So, yes, you can be happy and content with little. Just because you're prospering doesn't mean you have to live extravagantly if you don't want to. If you want a small house, God doesn't mind. Enjoy your little place. Be happy! Just make sure you bless others, too.

If you want a large house, God doesn't have a problem with that either. Build yourself a big one and don't wrestle with guilt. Enjoy what God has given you! Be happy! Just make sure that you bless others, too.

You've got to understand that God is not as interested in what you have as other people might be! That could be a revelation to you if you've been struggling with guilt. Remind yourself that *God doesn't mind you having things, just as long as things don't have you.*

## The Love of Money

It is the *love of money* that is the root of all evil, not money itself (1 Timothy 6:10). And there are many people out there who have a fierce love of money who don't have much of it in the bank. People always think it's the rich guy who loves money. But how many average or lower income people do you know who absolutely love money? How many of them talk incessantly about it? How many go on and on about what they'd do if they had it? I'd venture to say millions. They come from all walks of life and all tax brackets.

Hey, we all like money. It puts food on the table. On top of that, it sends the Gospel to the four corners of the earth. But money isn't the most important thing in life. People are. Money is just a means to bless more people with the goodness of God.

God doesn't have a problem with material things. He's filled His home in heaven with beautiful things, so that itself should tell you He likes nice stuff! But His priorities are in order: He cares more about people than houses and chariots. And so should you.

## Don't Get Caught *Not* Believing in Prosperity!

It just makes sense. If you've got more, then you've got more to give. By accepting that it is God's will that you prosper and by using the principles in His Word to obtain prosperity, you will have more to sow into different outreaches who are establishing God's covenant throughout the earth. There is nothing fleshly about giving or spreading the Gospel. It is what money is for!

If you deliberately choose *not* to put His principles for prosperity to work in your life, you can consider yourself just plain selfish. Why? Because you will deprive someone of the opportunity of hearing about Jesus! And you'll deprive yourself of the rewards in heaven. So, don't get caught *not* believing in prosperity. It could mean life or death to someone else.

If you're financially satisfied, don't stop implementing God's principles for giving in your life. Use the ideas He's given you to create wealth anyway. Do it with the intention of blessing others! Meanwhile, God will pour out more blessings to you. And if you don't want them, sow them!

On the other hand, if you aren't where you want to be financially, He'll supply all your needs and wants because you will be fulfilling His needs and wants, which are souls and more souls! **Seek ye first the kingdom of God, and his righteousness; and all these things shall be added unto you** (Matthew 6:33, Luke12:31). In other words, "Put Me first. Win souls for My kingdom, and I'll bless you with all those earthly things that you want." This is God's way. And you can't go wrong with God!

## Thinking God's Way

If you think of prosperity in terms of how much you can give instead of how much you can heap up, then you have God's perspective on prosperity. If you can think of prosperity in terms of souls, then you have God's perspective on prosperity. You're thinking like He thinks!

So maybe you've heard all your life that prosperity is in terms of your spiritual life only. And maybe you have a hard time believing otherwise. If this is the case, then you are going to have to re-condition your mind to think otherwise. **And be not conformed to this world: but be ye transformed by the renewing of your mind, that ye may prove what is that good, and acceptable, and perfect, will of God** (Romans 12:2).

Remember, just because you grew up thinking one way doesn't mean it's the right way. How many people were taught that the earth was flat before Christopher Columbus proved otherwise? Really, Job said it was round way before Columbus did. (Job 37:12.) Job just didn't get the credit because he got his information from God and didn't get in a boat and prove it himself. Isn't it amazing to what extent the world will go to avoid God's Word? (Makes you think, doesn't it?)

To be honest with you, I personally was taught so much trash that it took lots of prayer, Bible reading and good teaching to get me into line with the Word! Who knows? It might take the same for you. I can almost guarantee that it will. But once you get to really know God and grasp His perspective on prosperity, there won't be a person on earth who will be able to steal it from you!

# Chapter Four
## Getting to Know God

What if you had a friend who always repeated the same thing to you, every time you saw him? Maybe he'd say something complimentary, something really nice, but for some reason he just had to say it each time you came around.

But to make matters worse, you could tell that this guy was just saying it out of obligation. It didn't seem to mean all that much, but for some reason he felt he just had to say it anyway. Would you say that friendship had good communication? No? Then let me ask you this: why do you think so many people pray that way?

Better yet, have you ever caught yourself praying mindlessly? Just spouting off what you heard somebody else say? What about going through the motions of prayer and repeating the same old things?

Oh, now I know I'm stepping on some toes...but hey, that's what this book is for, to help you see beyond religion and into relationship. God is real. His Son, Jesus, is real. So, why do so many pray like He isn't?

## Do You Pray Just to See Where the Words Splatter?

You see, when somebody aimlessly prays a prayer I say that they are "spouting off" prayers. It's almost like people gather up all the good-sounding words they've heard and then spout 'em off. They pray just to see where the words may splatter.

But I don't believe God gets much enjoyment hearing His children spout off somebody else's words...especially when they do it just because they feel they have to.

What about you? Have you ever found yourself doing that? And ask yourself this: do you think God enjoys hearing His kids splatter words at Him that they don't really believe? No way! We've got to give God a little more credit than that!

Here's a one-liner I heard and I had to shove in here: "Many people give God credit, but very few give Him cash!" Ha! Isn't that the truth?!

Spouting off that kind of insincere prayer is like shooting dice. You hope that you get lucky and win the answer to your prayers but figure it's a game of chance and you've got a fifty/fifty shot. Prayers that sound good but have no personal meaning don't bring about a manifestation because there isn't faith involved. And faith is what brings the answer home to you!

All God is asking for is for you to put forth a little effort! All He wants is for you to desire Him and think about Him enough to want to talk to Him. He wants to hear your voice. But not just your voice; He wants to hear your heart. He's willing to share His true self with you. Are you willing to do the same with Him?

## What? Do You Think God Speaks Japanese?

God loves me. He just can't help Himself. Sometimes people think I'm arrogant when I say that, but I know it's true. God told me! He just loves me and He loves to tell me so. He speaks my language, and sometimes that's Cajun slang! Sometimes He talks sternly to me and sometimes He talks softly. But most all of the time He talks to me straight out, real and to the point. Why do you think He talks that way to me? Because that's how I can understand it.

I used to think He talked to everybody that way. But I've come to know that He doesn't. He talks to each individual in the way that he or she can understand Him plainly. Why? Because He doesn't want to make it hard for you! Imagine if I started talking to God and I said, "Hey, Jesus!" and He responded in Japanese. Would I be able to understand Him? No, I'm a Cajun! God speaks Japanese to a Japanese person. To me, it's Cajun!

But then what if I woke up in the morning and said "Hey, Jesus!" and He responded in this flowery speech that went something like, "Greetings to thee also, My son. How art thou this fine morn?" I would understand what He said, but if He started really trying to explain a situation to me and continued to speak flowery words to me it wouldn't be as easy to understand as a simple, "Hey, Jesse! Let me tell you what I want you to do today."

The Lord makes every effort to speak your language. He's holy and pure, so His words will only be holy and pure. But He will come across in a way that you can easily understand Him.

## Be Real!

What about you? Do you make every effort to be real when you're talking to Jesus? Or do you go digging in the back of your brain for the last good-sounding prayer somebody else said? How do you talk to Jesus?

How you pray when you are alone is probably a reflection of how your relationship with Jesus is. Do you talk to Him from your heart? Are you expecting to hear His voice? Do you pray like He is way up in the sky, almost out of reach? Or do you pray like He is right there in front of you, listening to what you're saying and waiting to respond?

Jesus is real! He is inside you and that is as close as He can get! So if He planted Himself right there on the inside of you, isn't it obvious that He wants to talk? Let me tell you something. God isn't interested in how holy and flowery you can sound. Unless you already speak eloquently and it's in your nature, forget about trying to sound good. Just be yourself. God already knows who you are. He made you. Remember, prayer isn't for Him to get to know you. Prayer is for *you* to get to know *Him!*

## God Will Shock Your Socks Off!

Maybe you are saved, but you really haven't developed an open, communicating relationship with Jesus quite yet. You might say that you've met Him and received Him as your Savior and Lord but maybe you have yet to experience that "friendship" type of relationship. You could be in that position no matter if you prayed the sinner's prayer two days ago or twenty years ago!

If that is where you are, man, are you in for a surprise! Once you start talking and being honest and real with God, you are going to find out that He is not the way you may have thought He was! God will shock your socks off! The more you read His Word and the more time you spend praising Him, you'll be astonished at how awesome and creative God is! Man, if I tried to explain just what I know about God, I'd run out of words before I could even begin to get it all out! And that's just what I know about Him!

His personality and nature is so multi-faceted, even the angels haven't seen all that He is! They continually fly over the throne shouting words of praise about Him as they see new aspects of His holiness! (Isaiah 6:2-3.)

Yet, for as complex and beyond our intellect as He is, it is amazing how simple He is to understand! When He talks to you, it won't be so beyond you that you can't understand Him. He's going to shoot straight with you and be real! You'll understand Him. He'll see to that!

All God requires of you is that you live a life that includes His Son, Jesus. He wants you to experience a full life on this earth, and the only way you can do that is first by accepting

His Son so that you can come back into right standing with Him and, second, by getting to know who He really is.

If you're ready to do that, then you're ready to experience all that God has to offer. You're ready to experience too much!

## Remind Yourself:
## Prayer Makes Life Easier. Doing It Isn't Hard!

Most Christians know that reading the Word and spending time with Jesus in prayer can help them. And in their hearts they might really want to do it. But somehow they become swept away with the day's "priorities" and become lazy when it comes to the Lord.

But you know, it really isn't such a big deal. You don't have to spend all your time on your knees, although you'll receive a lot of wisdom and insight doing that! What God really wants is for you to talk to Him. Wake up in the morning and do like I do. Say, "Hello Jesus!" Chat with Him throughout your day and you'll be able to keep a good relationship with Him. As you practice chatting and praying with Jesus each day, you'll find that you suddenly have the urge to find out even more about Him. He's just that way. Sort of infectious, you might say. It seems like the more you talk to Jesus, the more you want to talk with Jesus.

It's like eating. Let's say you're an average-sized person who makes a point of eating regular, wholesome, nutritious meals. Your body warns you when it is hungry by sending hunger pangs. But let's say that one day you decide to ignore your body and not eat. You miss breakfast, you miss lunch. By the time dinner rolls around, your stomach is growling at you like a tiger! But instead of eating, you ignore it again. If you keep on ignoring your body for a couple of days or more, your stomach will become accustomed to deprivation and may send you into a fasting state where the hunger pangs aren't nearly as frequent. You might not even realize that you are slowly but surely using up all the nutrition you need to stay healthy. If you continue fasting too long your health may decline without your really knowing it at all.

It's the same way with Jesus. Your spirit needs to have conversation with its Maker. It's a sort of built-in mechanism. Just as your body needs food to survive, so your spirit needs interaction with your Maker in order to survive.

## Go for the Good Stuff!

But what if your mind is empty and your will is idle because of it? Where does that leave you? Without results, that's where! Without a manifestation of God's awesome power to do "exceeding abundantly above all that you ask or think!" And you don't want that! Nobody wants that!

Nobody who knows what faith in God can do wants to live without His power in their lives. Most people just get carried away with life and neglect what is most important. They are sort of like Martha, worrying about food instead of sitting with her sister at the feet of Jesus where she belonged. (Luke 10:38-42.)

Next time you find yourself skipping prayer — even if you think you've got a great reason — think about Martha. Remember what Jesus told her: **Martha, Martha, thou art careful and troubled about many things: but one thing is**

**needful: and Mary hath chosen that good part, which shall not be taken away from her** (Luke 10:41-42).

You know, everything we do is important. But it isn't so important that we forget about ourselves. Talking to God doesn't take an hour a day! That's religious! How about you talk to him throughout your day? You have to cook dinner? So pray while you cook! Maybe you wake up late and have to rush to get dressed before flying out the door and hitting the freeway. So what! Does that give you a reason *not* to talk to God? Give me a break! C'mon! Forget about singing along with your car radio this morning! Instead, sing to Jesus! Or how about this: break out a good teaching tape and fill your mind with the good things! Hey, after all that rushing around, I guarantee you'll need it. If not, you might find yourself in flesh, blowing the horn and hollering at the next guy who whips out in front of you.

Look, no matter what you do or how busy you are at doing it, prayer ought not to be neglected. God's Word shouldn't be neglected. And neither should you neglect yourself. After all, prayer isn't really hard. It doesn't take all day. All it takes is honesty, no matter what you're doing. So, forget about cheating yourself! Go for prayer! It's the good stuff! Get to know God!

# Chapter Five
# **What Does "Too Much" Mean?**

Remember back in the Old Testament when Moses was try-ing to build the tabernacle in Israel? I love to read how God moved upon the hearts of Moses and the people to give into that building fund. They really got into it! What I think is great is how Moses didn't have to beg them to be a part of it. He didn't have a pledge drive or offer to print the names of every person giving twenty pieces of silver on a plaque and hang it in the foyer of the new tabernacle. These people *wanted* to give toward the tabernacle and they didn't need any incentive to do it! In fact, Exodus 36:5-7 says that Moses had to tell them, "Stop giving! Stop giving! We have *too much* already!" (Author's paraphrase.) Now, when was the last time you heard a preacher say that?

In Genesis 33, we read that years and years after Jacob had stolen his brother Esau's birthright and skipped town, he met up again with Esau. And even though he'd experienced pay-back in more than one way since then, he was still worried about confronting his brother.

So when Esau approached Jacob, Jacob presented him with a wonderful and generous gift. But instead of accepting his brother's gift, Esau declined and said, "Jacob, I'm a rich man. I have enough." (Genesis 33:9, author's paraphrase.)

But do you know what Jacob said? He replied, "No, brother, take it. I have it *all*." He didn't say he was rich. He didn't say he had enough. He said, "I have it *all*." There are two different Hebrew words translated "enough" here. In verse 9, the word Esau used means "abundant." In verse 11, the word Jacob used means "all" or "the whole." Jacob's simple statement proved what the Old Testament blessing of God could do. It made the difference between Esau's "enough" and Jacob's "too much!" It was the difference the blessing of Abraham made.

Now, what does "all" mean where you live? I'll tell you what it means in Louisiana. It means there ain't no more! God blessed Jacob until he had more than enough. The boy had too much!

Since Jesus has come into the picture, every believer in the world now has the right to receive God's *too much* blessings! Not just in the financial realm, but in areas much more significant than that! Think about it. God's plan of salvation is *too much!* And His grace? *Too much!* His mercy? *Too much!* His peace? *Too much!* His love? *Too much!* Think of any one thing that God has given to His children and you'll find that He always gives *too much!*

## God's Abundance Is Everywhere

The God of Too Much. You can go all through the Bible and find stories about Him. His abundant nature is evident everywhere.

When Deuteronomy 8:18 says **But thou shalt remember the LORD thy God: for it is he that giveth thee power to get wealth,** it's talking about two things: power and wealth. God's got the wealth. He's given you the power. Put them two together and you can touch the world!

Back in Joshua 19:9 (NKJV) you'll find that the children of Judah had so much "too much" that instead of heaping it up, they decided to bless the children of Simeon. It says that **the inheritance of the children of Simeon was included in the share of the children of Judah for the share of the children of Judah was too much for them. Therefore the children of Simeon had their inheritance within the inheritance of that people.**

Then you can skip over to 1 Kings 17:8-16 and find a little widow woman living during a terrible drought. "Elijah," she says, "I know you want me to fetch you some bread and water. But all I've got is enough flour to make one lousy pancake. After that, my son and I are gonna die from starvation. But since you ask me for it and since you've told me that God will supply my needs during this drought, I'll give you my last meal and I'll believe that what you say is true." (Author's paraphrase.)

Could you see what the media would say to that? They'd freak out! They'd print something like, "EVANGELIST TAKES LAST MEAL FROM LITTLE OLD WIDOW." They'd have a field day with Elijah! But you know the story. That widow's faith in the prophet of God caused a miracle to happen! Her jar didn't run out of oil and her bin didn't run out of flour. If you read some commentaries, you'll find out that it is believed the widow fed the whole neighborhood during the drought. Now, that's a lot of flapjacks. That widow sowed her "not enough" and got more than enough! Too much!

I love what Psalm 34:9-10 (NKJV) says: **Oh, fear the LORD, you His saints! There is no want to those who fear Him. The young lions lack and suffer hunger; but those who seek the Lord shall not lack any good thing.** How would you like to get to a point where you can say, "I don't lack any good thing, so I have no wants." Now, that's too much!

Then there is Proverbs 10:22 (NKJV): **The blessing of the LORD makes one rich, and He adds no sorrow with it**. When God blesses you there isn't any sorrow. No strings attached to make you weary. Nothing but blessing!

How about Isaiah 64:4 (NKJV)? **For since the beginning of the world men have not heard nor perceived by the ear, nor has the eye seen any God besides You, Who acts for the one who waits for Him.** Ears haven't heard and eyes haven't seen any other God who does what our God does for His children. That's too much!

Consider Jeremiah 32:27 (NKJV). **"Behold, I am the LORD, the God of all flesh. Is there anything too hard for Me?"** Now, that's a loaded question! Ask yourself that one and see if you don't all of a sudden realize the potential of believing The God of Too Much. Do you think it's too hard for Him to bless you with finances, to heal your body or save your family? Is it too hard for Him? No! "God is able to do exceeding, abundantly above all that you ask or think **according to the power that worketh in you.**" It's up to you!

Look at John 15:7: **If ye abide in me, and my words abide in you, ye shall ask what ye will, and it shall be done unto**

**you.** What things will He add to you? Anything! If He hasn't been adding to your life then maybe you haven't been seeking! Check yourself.

Now go to Matthew19:29 (NKJV): **And everyone who has left houses or brothers or sisters or father or mother or wife or children or lands, for My name's sake, shall receive a hundredfold, and inherit eternal life.** Wow! Now, that's too much. One hundred times your investment *and* eternal life? Your mind can hardly conceive being guaranteed the one-hundred-fold return, let alone adding life without end. Amazing. Too much!

And how about 2 Corinthians 9:8 (NKJV): **And God is able to make all grace abound toward you, that you, always having all sufficiency in all things, may have an abundance for every good work.**

Do you believe that God can do it? Can He give you an abundance for every good work? Is He omnipotent? Or impotent?!

## God Is Not Omnipotent in Heaven and Impotent on the Earth!

If God is omnipotent in Heaven, then He's omnipotent on the earth! He isn't impotent! He can do the things He says! We can have the things He says He can do!

If you believe it, then you ought to live it. If you believe in salvation you ought to be saved. If you believe in healing you ought to be healed. If you believe in prosperity you ought to be prosperous!

For years in my ministry, I made it a point not to spend too much time taking up the offering. I'd just say a little prayer and tell the people to give whatever the Lord laid on their heart and go on to something else. I thought I was doing good by spending only a few minutes on the offering. Everybody knew I wasn't a beggar and I felt good about agreeing with them! But one day the Lord set me straight about the two-minute offerings I'd been doing for years. He said, "Jesse, when you preach for an hour on salvation you expect people to come forward and be saved. And when you preach for an hour on healing you expect people to receive their healing. Why is it that you spend only two minutes on the offering when you know how bad my people need to be blessed?"

Whew! God gave me a revelation quick! And I knew it was time for me to change! This revelation is why I now take more time preaching on God's view of prosperity. People need to be debt-free! People need to be blessed spiritually, physically *and* financially! Why? So they can have enough for themselves and for every good work, so they can in turn be a blessing to *all* the families of the earth. (See 2 Corinthians 9:8; Genesis 12:3; 28:14.)

## Yes, You *Are* Worthy!

I used to have a real hard time receiving from God. I would give, give and give but I always seemed to feel guilty about receiving anything in return. Of course, I'd had a lifetime of "you're not worthy" stuck in my head and that's probably the main reason why. But there were a few other reasons too. One of them is what I can now call "the fear of men." (Isaiah 51:7; Psalm 31:19.)

The first time God really blessed me with abundance, I took about five steps back and said, "Whoa, God. I'm not worthy. Really, Lord. I'm really not worthy. You can't give me this. I just can't take it."

But He just said, "Enjoy yourself."

I said, "Oh...but I can't. People are going to talk, Lord. Are you sure about this?"

"Well, I wouldn't give it to you if I weren't sure. Go ahead, enjoy it," He replied.

I'd always loved blessing others. But when it came down to me I'd think, "Oh, I can't take this. I'm a minister of the Gospel and people worry about how much material stuff we have. I can't have anything like *that*. I'm a preacher."

And do you know what? It took me a while before I could receive with a good heart. Chipping away at that old religious mind-set could have been much harder had God not given me a good reprimand, though. And you know, it took that reprimand from God to convince me that I really was worthy of receiving financial blessing.

He made me see that I should be blessed not just because of anything I'd done, but because of what *Jesus* had done! He made me worthy through His blood. And preacher or no preacher, I'm now entitled to everything that blood bought!

If you're not a minister, you might not understand what a liberation that is. Let me explain. You see, if you're a preacher, people are always eyeing what you've got. They want to know how much money you make, what kind of car you drive, where you got your shoes and what's in your fridge! Unless you're dirt poor and struggling with an illness, it seems like everybody thinks you're a slimeball! And that can wear on you. It's like being convicted daily when you haven't done anything wrong.

People always cock their head back, sneer and say, "How much did you pay for that, Reverend?" insinuating that I must be a crook if I've got something nice. Many times I'd find myself trying to convince them that I'm "one of the good ones." When they sarcastically say, "Oh, isn't that nice?" I knew they really meant "You must have spent a bundle, Reverend. I wonder where you got that kind of dough?" Then I'd find myself stuttering, "Uh, uh, well thanks. I got it on sale. Fifty percent off!"

What I really wanted to say was, "Oh, that old thing? My wife got that at the junk yard down the street from our run-down shack. But she's handy. She slapped a coat of discontinued paint on it, tightened a few rusty screws with a ten-year-old butter knife and well, there it is! Nice, huh?"

But one day the Lord reprimanded me for talking and thinking like that. It was just after someone had questioned me about something materialistic and I was feeling kind of guilty for having something so nice. In the middle of my pity party the Lord said, "Jesse, what are you doing? Just tell them I gave it to you. If they have any problems tell them to come talk to Me about it! Don't you *ever* make an excuse for My blessings in your life!"

And it has been my motto on prosperity ever since: *never make an excuse for the blessings of God in your life*. It's exactly what the Lord told me to do and I don't feel bad about obeying Him. I'm not a greedy man and I'm no crook. Nobody can make me feel guilty for God's blessings. I'm a giver, so I'm bound to be a receiver! I love to bless others and I love to be blessed! And there ain't a devil in hell who's going to make me feel guilty for going out in the field and gathering up my harvest!

I love what a good friend of mine says when somebody asks him, "How much money do you make?" He is a minister just like me and he always says, "I don't make money. I live by my giving. What I sow is what I reap. Don't get mad at me if I'm blessed. I can't help it, I just keep on sowing and I just keep on reaping. My heavenly Father meets all my needs according to His riches in glory." That is so true and I love it so much that I've adopted my friend's reply as my own. I live by my giving! I sow and I reap! I can't out-give God because He's too much! Of course I'm blessed! How could I not be? Just look at Who my Dad is!

## When You Get Too Much of God Poverty Has No Place in Your Life

About seven or eight years ago, God gave me a little extra money. I had been believing for money for a project and more came in than I needed. So I had a little extra money and I had done everything He wanted me to do with it.

Now, most people would take that money and put it in a bank account. They'd let it make some interest and use it when the next need or project came along.

Of course, there's nothing wrong with that! But during this time I was studying  the  blessings of serving The God of Too Much and it dawned on me that I had just received too much!

That may sound simple, but it was a revelation to me. And I was excited about it.

Thinking about that extra money, I began to pray. "Lord, I don't need this. Now, what do you want me to do with this extra money?" The spirit immediately spoke up on the inside of me and said, "The reason why I gave you extra is because I don't just want to be a supply to you, I want to use you as a supply house for others."

"What do you mean?" I asked.

He said, "I gave you too much simply because I know that when a need rises before you, you will minister to that need for Me."

It wasn't more than three hours later that a person who had a desperate need was in my office. And there I was, able to meet the need with my "too much."

Now, I didn't ask God what He wanted me to do with it because I couldn't find a way to use that money. I'm sure that if I sat down and thought about it, even though it wouldn't have been in God's plan, I could have found somewhere to put that money. Who couldn't? But I didn't do that. And consequently I was able to meet somebody else's need when it arose.

When the man asked me why I was giving him the money, I told him, "I've accomplished what God wanted me to do since I began believing him to meet my need. But while I was waiting for the next plan to come through, I got this extra money. And it isn't enough to meet my next need. But it is more than enough to meet your need. Your need is before my eyes, so here." I handed him the money and he was thrilled.

"But that's more than I need," he said. "Share it with somebody. You'll meet somebody who has a need."

## Sowing Works!

See, every time you sow a seed, a harvest comes. The question is whether you go and get it. Very little seed will grow and produce a harvest if you neglect it out there in the fields. In the natural you know that there are all kinds of situations that can happen to ruin a harvest. It's only a well-cultivated garden that will yield the most produce. (Mark 4:1-32.)

The same is true with prosperity.

God is always more than enough. He always gives too much. That's just His nature. It is our job to keep the Devil from stealing our seeds by first naming our seed (so that we know what we're planting), sowing into fertile soil (so that we will reap the maximum-fold return on our giving), watering it with the Word and the words of our mouth (so that we can nurture and fertilize the seed during the growing time) and then harvest our harvest!

Is one part of the sowing process more important than the other? No! Each part is vital and none can work well alone. Think about it. If you just sow, but you don't name your seed, how will you know your harvest when it springs up? If you continually sow into poor soil, how do you expect to reap an abundant harvest?

And if you confess the words of prosperity over your life but do not sow, how can you expect to receive anything at all? The laws of sowing and reaping all work together for your benefit. It is God's way of ensuring that you receive too much.

Do you know that we don't experience "summer slumps" within this ministry? That's right, unlike many ministries our finances don't go to the dogs the minute summer comes around. It doesn't matter how busy people get after kids get out of school or how many of our partners go on vacation during the summer. We still don't have financial slumps.

And the reason is simple: we plant all year round! So we get a harvest all year round! I'm planting like crazy! Jesus makes my seeds grow, but I apply the principles according to His Word.

Sowing works in every facet because God is omnipotent. He knows *no* limitations. He doesn't put a cap on sowing. He doesn't say, "Well, now once you get to sowing such and such, I can only give you a five-fold return." No! It is thirty-, sixty- and one-hundred-fold! God's resources are vast! He knows no limitation! He isn't omnipotent in heaven and impotent in you. He turns His vast resources to your account. They are available to you. All you have to do to make a withdrawal on those resources is to exercise the laws that govern sowing and reaping in your life.

Those laws didn't come about after the fall of man. They were instituted way before that. Adam and Eve worked according to those laws before the fall. And God Himself continues to live by them today. Think about it: He sowed one Son and now has millions of sons.

## Can You Say "Amen!" When He Digs Into Your Pocketbook?

I'll never forget the first time God asked me to give a major chunk of change in the offering. It was at a Kenneth Hagin camp meeting. I'll never forget it. The offering was about to be taken up and Brother Hagin was speaking.

The Lord told me, "Now I want you to give ten thousand."

"Ten thousand!"

Man, when He said that, it shocked me! My toe would shake a little just letting go of a dollar. But ten grand? It felt like I was sitting in the electric chair! It wasn't the Holy Ghost though. It was just plain fear of losing my money!

Right after I heard God tell me to give $10,000 to Kenneth Hagin's ministry, a man leaned over to me and said, "You know, I just heard God. I believe God just told me to give $10,000."

I exhaled and smiled at him gratefully. "I heard it too," I said, figuring that I'd just overheard God telling this guy to give $10,000 and I was just his confirmation. Wrong! God told me again. That night He told us both to give ten grand apiece! And we obeyed!

First I thought, "Let me get out of here, man!" But I didn't, and the Lord blessed us back so much. He gave us television equipment and made the way for us to be on television ministering the Word of God. And at that time, there was no way we could have done it for $10,000. No way possible. But God used me to further the kingdom in another man's ministry, and then He gave me what I needed to further the kingdom through this ministry. I fulfilled another man's dream, and so He fulfilled mine. He provided seed to the sower, which was me. (2 Corinthians 9:10.) And He paid me back a serious return on my giving.

It's through experiences like that one that I've come to know that we should never be afraid of expecting great things from the Lord. He is faithful! And He'll not be a debtor. He is able to provide more than enough to meet the need! We know that *God is able to do more than we can ask or think according to the power at work in us!*

First Corinthians 2:9 says, **Eye hath not seen, nor ear heard, neither have entered into the heart of man, the things which God hath prepared for them that love him.** See, the religious world out there is worried about you expecting great things from the Lord. They think you are going to get in the flesh with it. But God has more confidence in you than that! So, never be afraid of expecting too much from the Lord. He isn't afraid to give it. Why should you be afraid to take it?

## God Can Follow Through, Now How About You?

God can follow through with prospering you. He can follow through with administering healing to your body. He can follow through with saving your lost loved ones. The question is: will you follow through with what God has told you to do in order to see all these things manifested in your life? The end of Ephesians 3:20 says that God will do what He's said **...according to the power that worketh in us.** That's right. The ball is in *our* court.

Essentially what it says is that God turns His vast resources to our account. It's up to us whether we will make a withdrawal or just stare at the numbers wishing we had what they stood for. Healing and prosperity are God's, but Jesus has deposited them into our account through His death and resurrection. Will we receive what He died to give us?

If we do, the Lord will keep on filling our account. When we start making withdrawals He'll heap more than we asked for into our hands. More healing, more prosperity, more peace!

Sure, the religious world will squawk! They'll try to condemn you for living a life of peace, joy, prosperity and health. They'll scowl, criticize and judge you. Why? Because they don't want you to have "too much!" They'd prefer it if you were broke, sick and full of worry, like them! Misery loves company, they say.

I've had some people get mad at me because it's been forever since I've been sick. The same ones get mad at me if I wear nice clothes or drive a nice car. And they get even more furious to see me smiling and happy, full of peace and joy, with a great marriage and a kid who is serving Jesus. Oh, it gets them mad to see me blessed with all that good stuff!

What they don't realize is that the same great stuff is available to them, too. It's sitting in their accounts right now waiting to be withdrawn! God gave Jesus a heaping helping of joy, peace, health and prosperity for each believer on the earth. Jesus deposited *too much* in each one of our accounts. Now, if we want it, we've got to make a withdrawal.

Don't get mad at me. I didn't say it, God did! He's able to do exceeding abundantly above all that you ask or think **according to the power that worketh in us.** Does it worketh? Yes! It worketh because it is God who gives us the power to make it work! What is that power? The Holy Ghost!

Language can't contain that power! Notice the difference between Peter's preaching before Pentecost, and his preaching after Pentecost. Before, maybe a few got saved. After, three to five thousand got saved! One sermon! What happened? He had too much! Too much of God! Notice that before Pentecost he was afraid. After the Holy Spirit had come, an angel had to kick him awake to get him out of jail because they're planning to kill him the next day. How many of you would be sleeping?

The power spoken of in Acts 2 is what transformed the disciples from a bunch of easily swayed believers to a group of Holy Ghost powerhouses who rocked the nations! It changed their lives and, if you'll let it, it'll change you, too!

## Chapter Six
# Godly Confidence Makes the Devil Nervous!

God never just fills a cup to the top, He causes it to runneth over! That's just His way. He isn't looking to give you just enough, He's looking to give you more than enough! So never be afraid to expect great things from the Lord. Doesn't 1 Corinthians 2:9 say, **Eye hath not seen, nor ear heard, neither have entered into the heart of man, the things which God hath prepared for them that love him?** He loves you! And His heart's desire is that you love Him too!

You know, I love the revivals of yesteryear. I've got books on the great revivals of the past and I read them to glean as much as I can from them. They inspire me and show me God's habit of waking up and shaking up generations of people. But as much as I love it, I don't live in it. I love what God did then, but I don't continue to try and revive those revivals of the past. Why? Because it won't change the future.

**...But this one thing I do, forgetting those things which are behind, and reaching forth unto those things which are**

**before...** (Philippians 3:13). There is a future in front of us. God is doing a new thing today. What was back then was wonderful but those revivals of the past won't meet the needs of the future. Why? Because the time has past. God has already done that and today He's going to move forward! **Behold, I will do a new thing; now it shall spring forth; shall ye not know it? I will even make a way in the wilderness, and rivers in the desert** (Isaiah 43:19).

That is why God wants us walking with Him daily, not living according to past religious history or living by the inspiration of yesterday. Not because what happened back then is wrong — it isn't — but the inspiration of yesterday is not sufficient for today. How the Holy Spirit moved decades or centuries ago was wonderful but the question is, how is He moving within *you* today? *You* determine that, not Him. You have a daily obligation to inspire yourself in the Word and allow the Holy One of Israel to use you.

You must inspire yourself daily by building yourself up in the Word. What does it say about you? Find out and let it sink in! When you know who you are in Jesus, you can look at a lost, sin-sick world with hope! You won't see them as hopeless because you'll know that there is enough Jesus inside of you to reach out to them all.

That is why it is so crucial that you really believe Ephesians 3:20. It is the main scriptural truth that I want you to walk away knowing in your heart after you've read this book. *God is able to do exceeding abundantly above all that you ask or think according to the power that works in you.* Believe that and you'll have boldness to do God's will in your life!

For example, a few years ago in South Africa a man told me, "You've got more boldness than anybody I've ever seen in my life!" Confidence in who I am in Jesus gives me boldness. Why? Because I know that when I walk into a room, I'm the most powerful person there! When I walk into a place, especially if it's a heathen place, I am the most powerful individual around. Why do I feel like that? Because I know Whom I serve! I know that my God is too much!

## Godly Confidence Gives You Boldness!

That kind of boldness and confidence makes the Devil nervous. He'll say, "Watch that Jesse! Watch him!" I love to aggravate the Devil! So sometimes I start walking up to a person, like I'm gonna talk to them, just to make the Devil nervous. When I get close to them, I don't say anything and the Devil looks like a fool! He gets all worked up over nothing and I think it's hysterical! He never knows what I'm going to do. And half the time, I don't know either.

If you walk into a room and folks are cursing, don't clam up. Do like I do, start praising! Man, I have walked into many a cussing session. In fact, I love getting around people who cuss because it gives me another opportunity to praise.

If you're a man and you've been to a health club where there is a men's dressing room or exercise section then you know how men can cuss! I don't know if it's the heavy weights or just that there aren't any women around to give men those disapproving looks, but it seems like when a bunch of guys get together, cuss words start flying.

When they crank-start the cussing motor, I just stand right by them and start praising. It's so funny to see their faces. Their foreheads crinkle up and they say, "What? What?" Then I repeat myself.

"Praise God!"

"Praise God?"

"Yeah! Praise the Lord! Glory! Thank you, Jesus!"

Suddenly they clam up on me. Suddenly, that weight machine way across the room starts looking awfully appealing. Some start backing away from me and making their way towards the far-off equipment. Others hang back and get quiet for a while. Then, the questions come. And that is when I have an opportunity to let my light shine and tell them a little about my life serving Jesus.

There is always that one guy who speaks up and says something like, "I don't believe in that blankety-blank-blank religious stuff!" That's when I get as bold as he is and say, "Well, glory to God! I do!!"

I don't care about being confronted! And neither should you! Why? Because the Greater One is living in you! Greater is He who is in me than he who is in the world! (1 John 4:4, author's paraphrase.) When I walk into a room, I'm the most powerful person there. I know it and the Devil does too! But that isn't so just because I'm bold. No matter who or how you are, if you're born again you're the most powerful person in the room.

What I think is funny is how after I start praising, most people immediately stop cussing. Either that or they leave the room! Haaa! Either way, the Holy Spirit takes control of that room and I can exercise without foul language annoying me.

Now, sometimes you have to deal with people who want to push you around. They enjoy confronting you just for the shock value. They want to see your face or what you're going to say when they continue cussing and start talking bad about God. In those situations, I just do a little shock treatment myself. Instead of falling into a theological argument, I just give them simple truths from the Bible in a very matter-of-fact way. I don't argue. I just give it to them straight. If I'm talking about accepting Jesus in order to go to heaven and they say, "Well, I don't believe in that." I just say, "That doesn't matter. Whether or not you choose to believe doesn't change the fact that it's true."

Then I start in with the facts. "Look, you have two choices, heaven or hell. That's it. There are no loopholes. If you say that you choose not to believe that there is a heaven or a hell, then you're saying that you don't accept this Bible as truth and you're calling God a liar. Which means that you also don't believe in His Son, Jesus. And your refusal to accept Him as your Savior is a choice that will send you to hell. But if you believe God's Word is Truth and you choose to receive Jesus into your life, then you've made a choice that will send you to heaven. So, heaven or hell, which will it be?"

In my own experiences, I've found that this kind of simple, no-nonsense approach works great with those who are confrontational and those who are into making up their own rules. I don't enter into any religious arguments. I just state the facts and ask them if they want to receive Jesus and go to heaven. If they don't get saved right then and there, at least I know that they've walked away having heard the Truth. From then on, they'll be accountable for it.

## For the Word's Sake

Sometimes, though, people can get really angry after hearing the Gospel. I'll never forget what happened years and years ago in Lafayette, Louisiana. I was preaching a sermon and this truck driver was sitting way in the back of the church. And man, this guy had some hair! He looked like a gigantic Brillo pad sitting there. Thick, wiry hair covered his arms and spewed out his unbuttoned shirt. I saw him sitting way in the back and he caught my attention because he was fidgety and looked real anxious. So there I was, preaching up a storm, when all of a sudden this wiry-haired man stood up.

In the middle of my sermon, he stood there and yelled, "I don't believe in that trash!" I stopped and looked at him. He was big. Real big. He must have stood six foot six, and he looked like he could easily weigh in at 350.

"Well come up here and see if it's real!" I heard myself yell back. I could hardly believe I had said that to this man. My mind was racing: *What did I say that for? What am I gonna do if he comes up here?* I looked at the pastor and I could see it in his eyes. *You're on your own, boy. I ain't jacking with this dude.*

I must have embarrassed the man by yelling back at him because right after I finished he jumped out of his row and angrily started making his way towards me. I'll never forget it because sweat was running down the back of my legs as I watched him strut towards me. In my mind I could see the headline in the newspaper, EVANGELIST DESTROYED BY HAIRY MAN.

Just then an old woman sitting near the front row caught my eye. She had begun to frantically pray in the Holy Spirit. From the fearful look on her face, it was obvious to me that everyone knew that as little as I was, I was no match for this man.

Suddenly, the Lord spoke to me and said, "When he gets to the second pew in front of you, I'll knock him down." When I heard that, my spirit went to praising. "Haaaaa! Come on, man! Walk faster!" But my body was still fearing for its life. And the sweat was still running.

"Sir," I said as he continued to walk, "when you get to this second pew you're gonna hit the ground like a brick."

"Yeah? We'll see," he growled back at me.

Now this church had a long, skinny sanctuary and as he kept on walking forward, passing pew after pew, I thought to myself, *Oh, if this church would only grow right now!* Then the man got to that second pew, and it was like somebody knocked him straight in the face! *Boom!* He hit the ground!

From the platform I yelled, "Haaaa, it worked!" The God of Too Much was protecting me! The man struggled a little and then stood up. "Wait!" he said and he reached out his hairy arm for me. When he did, *Bam!* He hit the ground again! "Don't mess with me, Mister," I said.

Obviously, the last supernatural punch shook him up because as he struggled to get up from the floor, tears began to well up in his eyes. "I need to get saved," I heard him say as he looked up at me from the floor.

I said to myself, *Thank you, Jesus. He needs to get saved.*

Well, we led that man to the Lord that night and he's my Covenant Partner today and I thank God for him. He's a real blessing of the Lord.

That night, I walked back to the hotel and the Lord said, "I noticed that sweat running down the back of your legs."

"Lord, I want to thank you," I said.

"Jesse, I'm not going to let anybody hurt you. I love you, Son."

"Thank you, Lord," I said. "But persecution comes for the Word's sake, huh?"

"That does happen sometimes," He said, "but if I would have let that man hit you, I would've had to raise you from the dead."

"Well, I sure appreciate it, Lord. Thank you."

"You're welcome," he said.

## Persecution Comes

That was a great one. But another time I was ministering, someone walked up and said, "I don't believe in your God." And then *whack!* He slapped me in the face! And he was only a little guy!

My face was burning. My anger was burning. The man had slapped me hard. I said to myself, "I don't need you for this one, God. I'm gonna kick this boy's brains out myself!" I looked at him and defiantly said, "You hit me?! You hit me?!" And I caught him by the shirt.

I couldn't believe he slapped me. I would rather he punch me because a slap is a real insult to a man.

My flesh reared up and egged me on, "Hit him, Jess! Hit him right between the eyes!"

I enthusiastically agreed. "I will and I'll repent tomorrow. But I'm gonna put my fist in this guy! You hit me?!"

Then I heard the Lord speak up on the inside of me, "They hit *me*."

I had this boy by the shirt and man, I was hot! I was furious! My Cajun blood was boiling in my veins as I heard the Lord again say, "They hit me, Jesse."

And again, "Jesse, they hit me."

My face was beet red and I was gritting my teeth and shaking with anger as I held this man by the shirt. "Let me tell you something, boy!" I snarled. About two inches from his face I hollered, "Ahhhhh, do you...know....Jesus?!"

"No," he sarcastically said.

"Let me give you some advice, boy! Repent now!"

I led that boy to the Lord but I didn't like it. I'm not sure whether he did it out of sincerity or out of fear. Either way, I didn't care. I went back to that hotel mad. "I tell you one thing, God! You let that little itty-bitty man slap me! Why...?! That was a little guy, God! A little guy!"

"Why didn't you turn the other cheek?" He asked.

"Because this one hurt! I didn't want any more! That's an insult!"

"You're well able to handle anything that comes your way."

See, I had to learn some things, and although God didn't send that guy to slap me, He did use it to teach me a lesson about persecution for the Word's sake. He used it to show me that just as He had been slapped, spit on, beaten and bruised for the Word's sake, there might come a time that I, too, would be persecuted because of my belief in Jesus and His Word.

## God Isn't a Terrorist

A few years ago, I had a very powerful organized crime leader's son get saved during one of my meetings. If I mentioned his father's name, you'd probably know him. He was in a major crime ring.

So, during the meeting the son got saved, gloriously saved by Jesus. After he had said the sinner's prayer, he came up to me and told me who he was. He was crying and patting me on the back saying," I love you. Understand what I mean, man? I love you." He was so sincere but really dramatic. He stared right in my eyes as he spoke to me and it made me kind of nervous. "Okay man, I love you too," I said, "Praise God!" He really was so blessed.

I left that town and traveled the rest of that year preaching the Gospel. During that time, I didn't think too much about the Mafia leader's son. But the next year I was scheduled to preach again in that area of New Jersey. This time, the son's father came to see me. He drove up to the front doors of the church in a big black limousine. The doors flew open and out stepped the father and a few other men, all of them dressed in suits. From the window in the church office, it looked like a scene from a Mafia movie!

The man walked right through the church doors and into the church office where I was waiting before service. He looked at me and, in a raspy New York accent, said, "I want to tell you something, Reverend. I want to thank you for what you did for my son. You understand?"

"Listen sir, I didn't do anything," I said. "You know, your son gave his life to Jesus. I just happened to be preaching that night and God blessed him." "Yeah," he said, "but he got off of drugs. Man, this kid's been nothing but trouble. I just want to say thank you."

I nodded my acceptance as he continued, "But, uh, my boss wants to talk to you."

Now his boss was I guess what you'd call the main man. He talked in a really raspy voice, sort of like the main guy in the Godfather movie. I was stunned as he said, "I want to tell you something. You did a favor for my associate's son and, uh, if you need anything you let me know. I'll help you out."

I could hardly believe all this as I answered, "Uh, I don't need anything."

"Well, let me say this, Reverend. We can do things you can't do. You understand?"

"Ummm," I said, "Well sir, I did nothing. Jesus Christ came in this man's life and saved his soul."

He waved his hand and casually said, Whatever. But let me just say this. If you call me, I can do some things for you that very few people can do. I appreciate what you did for my associate's son and thank you very much." He shook my hand as I said, "You're welcome."

He and his men left. They walked right out the front doors, climbed into the limousine and sped off. I was shocked. It was almost kind of funny to me. I stood there smiling because I felt like I'd just stepped out of a Mafia movie. It was great!

Well, as the Devil would have it, about two weeks later I found out that some church leaders were talking ugly about me. What I wanted to do was call up my new Mafia friend. In my best Marlon Brando imitation I wanted to say, "I want to tell you something. I want you to get some responsible people here. I want you to send them over to these people. Don't kill 'em, just break their legs, knock a few arms off. Take care of the situation and tell them, 'Don't mess with Jess.' "

That's what I felt like doing! And you know, I believe if I would have called them they would not have had a problem with that. But I can't do that! Why? Because that's terrorism! Hollywood has glamorized crime. They glamorize its leaders and make them into heroes.

It's a sad thing, but I see many people today who live the same way with God. They say they believe God is good, but secretly they still harbor those old religious ideas that God could hit them with a catastrophe or disease at any moment.

God isn't a terrorist. He isn't part of the Mafia. He's good. Really good. And He's waiting on you to trust Him completely. Are you ready to do that? Are you ready to have hope? To use your faith? To see the impossible become possible with God?

This isn't hype, you know. Faith in God is real. Faith in God can change a dull, miserable life into an adventure! There's nothing like trusting God to get your blood pumping. If you've stepped out in faith before, then you'll know what I mean. It's exciting to have a good attitude and really know that God will come through! It's exciting to move into action and see His plan come to pass in your life.

Faith is fun. Let's learn more about it! Turn to the next chapter!

## Chapter Seven
# Attitude and Action:
# The Ingredients of Faith

When faith is mixed in your life, life will become an adventure! When you start trusting God with your life, watch out! Adventure is coming to you! You never know what good things will happen. God loves to surprise His kids with good stuff.

But if we want to use faith and see things happen, we're going to have to learn how. And I've found out that there are two important things that you must have in order to use faith to the fullest. I call it the two-fold constitution of faith. I call it that because I think of faith as God's way of getting things done on earth. It's sort of His constitution.

Attitude is the first vital part of faith. When you look to the Spirit of God for direction, you must have a positive attitude. You must speak good, faith-filled things and repeat what the Scriptures say if you want the power of faith to work for you. This is the confessing part.

Action is the second vital part of faith. That's when you receive the direction from the Spirit of God and act on it! You cannot just talk. You must act on the Word. This is the possessing part of faith.

If you mix attitude and action in your faith you can produce any manifestation that you desire in this life, provided you have a deep sense of need and a strong hope of supply.

## Get Up and Go!

Faith is an adventure. But you won't be going on any adventure by just talking about it. You've got to get up and go! You can confess until you are blue in the face, but if you don't reach out there and possess what God has given you, you won't have it. Try mixing that confession with possession and you'll see something happen! Just like attitude and action, confession and possession work together. You really can't separate them at all.

Hebrews 11:1 says, **Now faith is the substance of things hoped for, the evidence of things not seen**. *Now!* Not tomorrow. Not next week. *Now faith is!* The church world has it mixed up. God is saying *Now faith is....* They are saying, "Is faith now?" Wrong. *Now faith is!* Get it?

When you're flat-out tired, when do you want to sleep? And when you're hungry, when do you want to eat? I don't know about you, but when I'm tired I want to sleep *now*. When I'm starving, I don't want to eat later. I want to chow down *now*! That's how faith is. It's now.

Thinking about eating makes me remember my Dad. Seems like Daddy was always hungry! When I was a small boy, I'd watch Daddy walk right up to Mama when she was in the kitchen frying up dinner. (Dinner, of course, was always fried or stewed because we lived in south Louisiana.)

Daddy would hug Mama, then steal a chicken leg off the plate beside the frying pot! Mama thought he was just being affectionate, but I saw what was up. He was hungry! I mean, if she caught him, which she did most the time, she'd fume! She'd holler at him until he scatted out of the kitchen.

You know, I don't understand what the big deal is with women. Why is it that it is soooo important that noooobody eats anything until it's all set out on the table? They don't want you touching a thing! You can't get a little taste of the fried chicken first. God forbid if you dip a spoon in the peas. God would have to tear off the throne before a woman in my family would let you sneak a bite. That's just how it is. And it's hard on men. Why? Because we want it *now! Now hunger is!*

I know a couple of men who love food so much they'd hug their wife and say, "Oh, I love you, sweetheart" while they slide a handful of mashed potatoes in their pants pocket! They'd go in the bathroom and lock the door just to eat it so their wife couldn't see!

See, just as much as you want that food now, so faith is! And you thought I was getting off the point, didn't you?

## Faith: It's Like Money in the Bank

When I begin to believe for something in my life, I use faith. I put faith on the line. I don't just stand around confessing. I put action behind my faith. I do everything in my power. God does everything in His power. I don't try to cross over into God's area.

I can't make it happen. But I can prepare the best way I know how for God to make it happen. I can do my part! God always does His. The finished product is a manifestation of whatever I was believing for.

It's when I combine action and a strong attitude of faith that I see manifestations coming. Before they ever get to me in the natural, I'm seeing them with my spirit. If I need something, I create an image in my mind of the finished product. I start talking like it's mine in the natural. God's doing it. It's like money in the bank.

See, my faith brings that manifestation to *now*. I see it now! Then, it makes no difference how long it takes to manifest in the natural, because I've already put my attitude and action in check. *I'm possessing.*

To me it's a done deal. And that's why it's never long before I see the manifestation in the natural come to pass. That may sound a little crazy if your mind isn't renewed to the Word. God never does things the way we think He should. Why? Because we're thinking with a natural mind and God, on the other hand, is supernatural. **For as the heavens are higher than the earth, so are my ways higher than your ways, and my thoughts than your thoughts** (Isaiah 55:9).

Our thinking needs to be renewed by the Word of God so that we can start thinking more like Him. Ephesians 5:26 says He will *sanctify and cleanse* you by the *washing of the water of the Word*. Grab that Bible and start scrubbing up that old crusty mind. Wash that baby with the Word of God until it sparkles likes Jesus' mind!

## God's Way Is the Right Way!

The first thing you have to accept is that God's way is the right way. He established the power of faith, so it works His way, not your way. If you want to see a manifestation of God's power in your life, you have to use faith His way. And that means renewing your mind so that you can start to think more like Him. You can't live by faith with an unrenewed mind. That's why time in the Word and time with the Lord in prayer is so important. They renew your mind so that you can fully grasp faith. If you don't take time to get to know the Lord, if you don't take time to renew your mind with His Word, then you will find yourself becoming double-minded, going back and forth between doubt and faith. And that's miserable! It isn't faith and it won't bring results!

So do you want to understand how faith really works? Great! Here it is: first you get a good attitude of belief. You believe with your heart until you can see that manifestation on the inside of you. Then, you act on your good attitude of faith by taking opportunities that God gives you. You don't sit around aimlessly waiting. You act by doing what you can in the natural, believing God through your prayers, actions and speech, and you allow Him to do what He can in the super-natural. Once you really believe and aren't aimlessly waiting (which is attitude without action), once you bring your faith into the now (with attitude *and* action), then the manifestation of what you've already been seeing with your spirit comes to fruition in the natural world. In a nutshell, that's faith!

Faith is knowing that you can't exhaust God's provision. Faith is knowing that God is too much! You know, every time I approach God I know He's gonna bless me with more than I can think or ask. I know it. I expect it. And that is why it happens. I'm not arrogant in myself. I'm confident in God! He's the one doing it all. I'm just obeying what He said.

In fact, I get ready for God's blessing. And yet I'm still not able to receive the full blessing of God. Why? Because it's too much! God astounds me! He just knocks my socks off! And when He does, I'm not afraid to let whoever is standing nearby know about it!

## Being Instant in Season and Out!

I don't know about you, but I find that I use spiritual phrases when I'm talking. I don't even think twice to say "Praise God!" or "Hallelujah!" if I'm in a restaurant. If people think I'm strange, it's no sweat off my back. When I was in the world I didn't care if you heard me cuss. Now that I'm saved, I don't care if you hear me praise. Pride is out the window when it comes to that. My pride comes from knowing God! It's only in God that I can boast. He gives me something to shout about!

That is why I'm not embarrassed to let people know that Jesus Christ rules and reigns in my life. I love to pray over my food. I don't mind doing it loud. I love it when waitresses come to the table and I say, "Would you like to pray over the food?" I love to see their faces. They go, "Ba, ba, ba, ba."

Sometimes I'll say, "You'll get a good tip." They get nervous and fumble over their words.

Honestly I've hardly ever had a waiter or waitress take me up on it. Mostly they just laugh nervously and thank me kindly. I end up teasing them to make the situation more comfortable. Still, I like to make them think a little. Come to think of it, the only time I can remember a waitress taking me up on my offer was in a greasy-spoon diner years ago. I'll never forget it.

It was one of those joints where they serve cholesterol by the pound. And the place was packed. This crazy waitress came walking up to the table where a pastor friend and I had just sat down. She was chomping on a mouthful of bubble gum, smacking with her mouth wide open and smiling at us as she approached the table. The woman looked like she was chewing tobacco! Her cheek was all bulged out and in my mind I could see her spewing a big black spitball on the floor. It was kind of funny.

"Ya'll know what ya'll want?" she asked as she threw down a table's worth of forks and knives. I looked down at the flatware and she said, "Pass 'em out!"

"Yes, ma'am," I said. Bless God, I never set a table before! Guess this was my night. So boy, I laid those forks and knives out as neat and orderly as I could, looked up at her when I finished and asked, "Whatcha got?"

"Everything," she said, smacking.

*That's everything greasy,* I thought. *But I'm gonna die with a smile on my face!*

I'll never forget that old girl. She reminded me of that red-headed waitress Flo on that old TV show in the 1970's,

"Alice." Do you remember that show? Flo had this big beehive hairdo and chomped on gum all the time. Anyway, this wait-ress reminded me of Flo, with her gum and her pen scribbling down orders on a tiny white pad.

Back then, I ate just about everything fried and with extra cheese. (I hadn't got a revelation about the connections between lard and sickness yet. Neither had the rest of the world.) So when the waitress asked what we wanted to eat I ordered a cheeseburger, fries and a plastic cup of Tab, the most bitter-tasting diet cola on the market at the time. Oh, yeah. I had to have a diet cola.

When our order was up, she slid those white platters of fat right on the table in front of us, hunkered down on the wad in her mouth and hollered, "Anything else?"

"Would you like to say the blessing?" I asked smiling, know-ing that most of them freak out. But this woman looked right at me, slurped up her gum juice and brazenly hollered, "Bow your heads!"

I was the one freaking out. I couldn't believe it! Between the gum-smacking and the breath-sucking, the "Thank ya, Jesus!" and the "Amen!" our food was *blessed!* And when she was finished, she just smiled at us and walked off.

The pastor looked at me and he said, "She blew you away, didn't she?"

"She did," I agreed.

Now, I'd call that waitress a woman with attitude and action! She smiled all over that joint and obviously didn't care if you knew she was saved. She didn't hesitate a minute to pray and wasn't looking over her shoulder to see if anyone was listening. She prayed to her God both in her heart and in the restaurant.

I learned something from that incident that I hope will help you too. For me, it was inspiration to see that woman totally uninhibited, being herself and boldly serving the Lord. She was instant in season and out! She had attitude and she was walking in action! Not a minute of hesitation. Yet, her personality was as alive as ever. That is how we should live, being true to ourselves and our God. Not acting like someone else, but letting God use our own individual personalities and gifts to serve Him. Walking in an attitude and action, with our personalities alive and our faith in full display.

## Receiving the Message of Faith

So let's go further with attitude and action. Let's learn how it can apply even more to your life. Now, how can we get a really good attitude of faith? Remember, God is not enough, He's too much! That's right! It's knowing in your heart that God really is too much. What happens when you really know something is true? How do you act when something is so concrete that it cannot and will not change?

I don't know about you, but when I'm in a place that is unchangeable and for my benefit, I act pretty confidently! When I feel certain about a situation I act as if it is already done. My attitude is confident and I take action because I'm certain that nothing is going to interfere with the end result.

You see, if we would all believe what I'm preaching here in this book, we would all be in heaven right now. I would be standing before the throne of God praising the maker of the universe. You would be there too. Not because this preaching is so good, but because mixing attitude and action speeds things up in the supernatural. Faith draws on the power that is in God. With our renewed mind, we line ourselves up with God's ways. This causes us to do His will more readily. And what is His will? That the Gospel of Jesus be preached to the entire world! That every man, woman and child hear and respond to the life-changing power of Jesus' blood!

We'd all have gone home with Jesus by now if every Christian really believed that God is too much. Too much love, too much redemption, too much healing, too much joy, too much prosperity...well, just too much "too much!" If people really believed that, they wouldn't hesitate to tell everyone they know about it. Who wouldn't want too much of a good thing? Who wouldn't want Jesus?

Today, it is time for all of us to receive the message that **God so loved the world, that he gave his only begotten Son, that whosoever believeth in him should not perish, but have everlasting life** (John 3:16). What did God do? He gave. He gave what was dearest to His heart simply because He loved people. He gave His Son, Jesus, and then He gave eternal life to all who would receive His Son. What generosity! What love!

We need to know in our hearts that God really is good. He's not slack and He's not withholding any good thing from us. It is time for us to receive the true nature of God and run with it to the world.

## I'm Gonna Be a Bride!

Years ago I learned something that was really eye-opening. You know, I got married years ago. I was the groom and Cathy was the bride. But today, I'm part of the bride (or body) of Christ! Kind of funny, huh? I'm not going to get into theological discussion about it but one thing I know for sure: I belong to Jesus and Jesus belongs to me!

Now this is sort of how it goes: Jesus is the Bridegroom and I (along with the rest of the saved world) am the bride. Together we walk to the throne of grace to see the One Who joined us together, God. We walk together in spirit but there will come a day when we will walk together physically. Why? So that we can begin the most glorious "honeymoon" ever, an eternal existence in heaven!

That is why Jesus said, **Surely I come quickly...** in Revelation 3:11, 22:7, and 22:20! Because according to God's timing, it's only been about two days. **But, beloved, be not ignorant of this one thing, that one day is with the LORD as a thousand years, and a thousand years as one day** (2 Peter 3:8).

It hasn't even been a weekend! Do you understand? To God, it hasn't been that long. Believe me, Jesus wants to see you as much as you want to see Him! He's ready now! But God is the One Who sets the appointed time. And He wants to make sure that the "bride" or "body" is as large as it can possibly be. He wants her fat!

When I married Cathy I didn't want to spend too much time hanging around and talking at the reception. I wanted to go! I wanted to get out of there pronto! People wanted to talk, but I didn't have talking on my mind. I was bent on getting out of that place!

"We're in a hurry," I'd say when they'd try to stop and talk some more.

"What are ya'll in a hurry for?"

"Uh...we've just got to go!"

You know what I'm talking about. When Cathy and I got in that car, I was zooming! I looked over at Cathy and said, "What's happening, Mama?" And I could see it in her eye, "Anything you want, Papa!"

Man, I was driving that car so fast I could have cared less if I'd gotten a ticket! If a cop would have stopped me, I would have hollered, "Give me the ticket quick! It's my wedding night, man! I gotta go!"

## Crock Pots and Microwaves
## Actions and Attitudes

That reminds me of what I once heard someone say: "Men are microwaves, women are crock pots." And isn't that the truth! This guy said all you have to do is press the right button and a man heats up quick. But a woman? You have to flip the switch and let her warm up before she'll get cooking. But when that crock pot gets hot, watch out! That pot will burn you! It's a scorcher! The problem here is that by the time the crock pot gets warm, the microwave has already gone off. Ding! Ding! Ding! It's finished!

Well, it's that way in the physical. But it can be applied to the spiritual. (You thought I got off track again, didn't you?)

The microwave is our action and the crock pot is our faith! Action is quick and does what it needs to do without hesitation. The attitude of faith is in it for the long haul! It's going to keep on heating until it has gotten whatever is in there cooked to **well done thou good and faithful servant** (Matthew 25:21-23). Now that'll preach!

## Are You Comfortable in God's Presence?

If you have an attitude of faith, then you are continually looking upward for guidance. You'll keep your eyes on Jesus. Practically, how do you keep your eyes on Jesus? Through fellowship with Him. Simply by praying and keeping your heart open to Him on a daily basis. (Not just on a Sunday basis — a daily basis!) If you keep yourself aware of the presence of God, then you'll be more in tune with His prompting and you'll be more confident taking action! You'll be walking the same path many of the most successful people of God throughout the ages have walked. You'll be walking by faith!

That is why I have a really hard time understanding people who say they don't believe in "that faith stuff." The Scripture says plainly enough, **But without faith it is impossible to please him: for he that cometh to God must believe that he is, and that he is a rewarder of them that diligently seek him** (Hebrews 11:6).

So if faith pleases God then what does lack of faith do? Well, I guess there is only one thing it can do _ it displeases God. Now that's strong, I know. But what many people who disregard faith are really saying is that they don't believe in pleasing God. And, to me, that simply means that if they are flatly refusing to please God, then they are living in disobedience to His Word. Whew! Strong, huh?

I believe that there is a reason for people vocally attacking faith. Of course, the Devil is blinding their eyes to the Truth because he doesn't want them to use the force of faith. But I want you to understand why Christians who don't use their faith always seem to be the ones who attack those of us who do. The reason is simple but true: *they aren't comfortable in the presence of God.*

There, I've said it! Now, if you're contemplating sending me an ugly letter, don't bother because I won't read it. Whenever I say this in a church meeting, people get real quiet. And they should. Contemplating what you are doing within your own life is good. Checking yourself to see if you have attacked or ignored faith is good. It's the only way you'll ever even notice what you're really doing.

## You Can't Be Comfortable in God's Presence If He's Displeased With You

And if you are attacking or ignoring faith in God, then He *is* displeased with you. Now, that's strong but it's true. And truth will set you free if you let it.

If you're not living in faith and standing by faith on the words given to you in the Bible, then when you get around God you feel sort of uncomfortable. You may not even realize why you feel this dead space when you pray. You may have been living without faith so long that you don't even realize that your relationship is uncomfortable. Instead, you might still be cuddling the religious blanket. Why do you think so many people feel like they aren't worthy to stand in the presence of God? Because they aren't comfortable in God's presence and it's easier to just say, "I'm not worthy. Oh, I'm a low-down dirty dog! I'm a piece of living trash. Oh, God, I need help!" instead of standing by faith.

So what happens when lack of faith in God creeps up in your life? You start retreating from God. You may avoid spending much time in prayer. Why? Because it isn't comfortable. You're not pleasing God. And inside your heart you know it. So what happens then? You start getting religious. You start praying prayers to the wind, not really believing (having faith) that God is going to do anything about your problems but feeling like you should pray about them anyway.

## What to Do About It

If you're in that situation, I don't have to tell you that you're lacking an intimate relationship with Jesus. But don't get discouraged. All it takes for you to change that situation is to notice where you went wrong, repent to the Lord in prayer and get right back into intimacy with the Lord. God isn't going to punish you for being away. The Devil might try to punish you for turning back to God, but God won't! The Lord's arms are open wide and He's ready to begin right where you left off!

I've heard many people say that it is cruel to tell someone that they lack faith. That's a lie. If you say it in love — that's the key — and if you genuinely want to help someone get back up on their faith-feet, there is nothing wrong with showing someone the Way. If it is cruel to say the words "lack of faith" to someone else, then Jesus was the cruelest man alive because all over the Gospel He continually says things like, "Oh, you people of little faith. How long must I suffer to be with you?" or "Why are you people so fearful?" Basically He's saying, "Listen to what I'm saying. Philip, Thomas, you asked me about the Father but you don't even know who I am."

## Jesus Wasn't Cruel

Now, Jesus was *never* a cruel individual. He was the exact opposite of that. He was loving, kind and concerned about the welfare of people. But He had enough love in Him to tell people where they were wrong. And most of the time it dealt with faith. And, man, Jesus was into faith! He talked about it a lot!

In Jesus' day most people who He said lacked faith were those who either didn't believe He was really God's Son or those who had a hard time accepting that the impossible was possible with God. Today it's the same way. Most people either don't believe that Jesus is the Son of God or they don't believe that He really will do something in their lives.

But you know, Jesus didn't tell them they had a lack of faith to cut them down and act like the big man, although He really was The Big Man. He said it so they would wake up and realize where the power was! Jesus saw the needs of those sick, miserable people. He knew that they desperately wanted God to intervene for them and that they just didn't know how to make it happen. He loved them and didn't want them to continue being lost, wandering sheep "baaaaing" all over town looking for relief. So what did He do? He told them where they were wrong and then He showed them the Way!

See, Jesus had an attitude of faith. He lived continually looking upward to His Father God for guidance and fellowship. And that's how He was able to tell the truth in a spirit of love.

You have that same spirit of love residing within you. In fact, you can have the same attitude and action of faith that Jesus has by opening your eyes and heart to Him. So what do you have to do to get it? Keep yourself aware of His presence. Walk in His commands. Make communicating with Jesus a habit.

How do you make those things habit? Practice! Practice waking up in the morning and starting your day like I do by saying, "Hello Jesus!" He's there, you know. He sees you pulling yourself from the bed, with your half-crumpled-up face and bad breath. He's watching you go to the sink and grab your toothbrush. He's watching you picking out your clothes from the closet and driving to work. Acknowledging the Lord's presence in your life takes faith. You have to believe that He's listening.

## Do You Think God Hears You Cuss?

What about you? Do you think God's listening to your prayers? When I think about those questions, I always think about cussing. Yeah, I do. I think about how funny it is that so many Christians are so scared to cuss out loud because they're scared God will hear them. They think that if they go *blankety-blank-blank-blank*, then God will hear them and send down that lightning bolt! *Wham!*

Those same people pray and pray and pray, and wonder if God is listening at all! Well, don't you think that if God can hear you cuss, then He can hear you pray? Think about it!

How many times have you said something that you think isn't right and you know without a shadow of a doubt that God heard it. Yeah, you can almost feel His eyes locked on you. Yet, how many times have you prayed about something and then thought to yourself, "I wonder if I got through? Well, maybe He's listening. Then again, maybe not." Come on! God hears it all! The cussing and the praying, the good and the bad — God hears it all! Whether you feel Him or not, His presence is ever present in your life!

## Acknowledge His Presence

Once you determine in your heart that He's there, why not acknowledge Him like I do first thing in the morning? And why not go a step further and actually acknowledge that He's with you throughout the day?! Why not keep up the communication throughout the day?

How do you keep up communication with the Lord throughout the day? By listening to Him speak through your spirit man and through the Word. I call that continually looking upward to God. You're aware of His presence and you're consulting Him throughout the day. Since you know that He's there and listening, you have somebody to lean on, to bounce problems and situations off during the day. You've got some comfort!

That is when the action of faith can come in. Since you're tuned into God and have your spiritual "ears" open, He can lead you much better than if He had to compete with everything else begging for your listening ears. He can steer you from a destructive path or quicken you to say or do something to help somebody else. But the best part is that you have someone Who will stand by your side no matter what happens. You have someone Who will never leave you or forsake you, Who will always be there to love on you when you need it. You have a reservoir of love, joy and wisdom just waiting to be tapped into.

That is God. And when you are communicating with Him daily, you're walking with faith, attitude and action! That is where the miracles are!

# Chapter Eight
## Knowing Jesus Isn't Dull

Knowing Jesus isn't dull. In fact, if you think about it, it's pretty exciting! Conversing with the maker of the universe? Whew! It's enough to blow your mind! Yet, it is amazing how many Christians don't really think of their relationship with the Lord that way. When I was lost and in the world I can't remember how many times dull and miserable-looking Christians tried to convert me.

They'd drone, "You need to meet Jesus Christ and make Him Lord of your life," in that nasal Southern monotone. Most of the Christians I met looked so sick, broke and bored that I felt sorry for *them*. I thought I should be converting *them!* Their lives didn't appeal to me at all! Most were fighting all kinds of afflictions — and they wanted me to get in the same boat with them!

If you happened to actually find Jesus through their witness, they'd let you in on how it was going to be, saying, "Now once you get born again the Devil will beat you and bust you.

He'll stomp on you, kick your head off, rip your skin off your back. So get ready, he's gonna get you soon! But remember, *he that endureth to the end shall be saved.*"

Well, they didn't say it quite like that. But close. Real close! That is just how it was when I was a young man. I used to think to myself, "Man, I'm gonna wait till the end! When I'm on my deathbed I'm going to ask Jesus to come into my life. I'll slide into heaven on a tight home run! Whoa! *Safe!* That way I won't have to get run over by the Devil."

It is a sad fact that most of the Christians I knew weren't living what they were preaching on Sunday. I'd hear them say, "God is love," and then criticize and fight with each other two seconds after service ended. I thought they were a bunch of hypocrites. "At least I do what I say," I'd reason to myself. I was thinking about sin, talking about sin and doing sin! No hypocrisy here! I was going to hell with gusto and figured that ought to count for something.

## Jesus Reached Out to Me

When I finally came to the end of my rope, I was a rock musician, doing drugs and drinking a fifth of whiskey a day. Yet the Lord cared enough about my soul that He put it on the hearts of caring Christians around the world to partner with Billy Graham Ministries. They put Dr. Graham on prime time national television and for that I'll be eternally grateful. Because it was through his televised crusade that I came miserable, weak God. He showed me a loving and merciful God who was strong enough to wipe the sin out of my heart and compassionate enough to take me just as I was. That night, before a gig in Boston, I walked into a little hotel bathroom and met God. I found out right then and there that He was not enough, He was too much.

It wasn't enough that Jesus came into my heart and saved my soul from hell. It wasn't enough that He lifted the weight off my calloused heart. It wasn't enough that He miraculously freed me from the addiction to alcohol and drugs. It wasn't just enough. It was too much! More love than I could grasp and more than I could use. God gave more than I could receive.

## Meeting Jesus on the Water

That's how God is. You don't have to beg God to perform His promises. All you have to do is accept them! They are there for the taking. Is your heart open for the receiving?

Remember Peter when he was on the boat and saw Jesus walking on the water? He said, "If that's you Lord, bid me to come." Peter wasn't expecting an answer. He thought it was a ghost! But Jesus said, "Come." And Peter looked at the rest of them in the boat and I bet he thought, "Did He just say what I thought He said?" The Bible says Peter got out of the boat.

That's what I'm talking about when I say that faith is a two-fold constitution. First is the attitude of faith. It was exemplified in Peter's request: "Jesus, if that is you, bid me to come." When Jesus responded by saying, "Come," He was essentially saying, "Now, Peter, walk in the faith that you have spoken." Peter then moved into the second part of the two-fold constitution of faith: action! He exemplified the action of faith by taking a step out of the boat.

See, after Jesus responded to Peter, Peter had a responsibility to own up to his own faith-filled words. The same is true for you and me. We have a responsibility to have an attitude of faith by saying, "If it's you Jesus, I will do this thing. I will meet you on the water." When He responds favorably, it is then our responsibility to move into action and do that thing which God has shown us. That is the two-fold constitution of faith. Attitude and action, saying and doing. You can't separate these two. You must have both working in your life to receive optimum results.

Taking that step out and doing something that isn't certain in the natural can be really unnerving if your eyes aren't fixed on Jesus. Focusing on the Lord is the only way to get through those situations, because your natural mind is going to try to protect itself! Your mind might be thinking, "You are some kind of fool thinking that you can walk on water! You're gonna sink, boy!"

That's what happened to Peter. He started looking at the water instead of Jesus and started doubting. And what does doubt do? You know. It stops faith from working. Peter sank because of that and Jesus had to pull him up so he wouldn't have to swim back to the boat.

But you know the wonderful thing about Jesus is that even if you do get your eyes off Him and end up falling in the water, He won't leave you there to drown. The Lord is out there with you and He is going to pick you up when you put your eyes back on Him!

You can't lose! When you make that first step toward Jesus, you are getting away from the religious crowd in the boat and you're stepping closer to God. If you mess up and fall in the water, He is out there with you, reaching out His hand. And either way you're still closer to Him than you were in the boat!

## If God Doesn't Meet My Need, He Doesn't Meet His Need

I had a minister tell me one time, "You know, I notice you've never had any financial trouble in your ministry."

I looked at him and said something that I think will help you better understand God's position in your life. I said, "Well, if God doesn't meet my need, He doesn't meet His need."

He said, "What do you mean?"

"I'll say the same thing that Paul said, except that I'll take it out of Philippians. I'll say *my* (meaning Jesse's) God will supply all my needs according to His riches in glory in Christ Jesus."

My God has needs. That's right, He has *my* needs. When I got saved He adopted me as His child and has become my El Shaddai, my Provider. That is why I feel comfortable in calling Him "My God!" Why? Because He *is* my God!

When Paul spoke of God, he got personal and also called Him "My God." He said, **My God shall supply all your need according to his riches in glory by Christ Jesus** (Philippians 4:19). Now did Paul have a need? What was his need? Well, nothing for himself. Everything Paul was doing was God's work!

The reason I feel so confident asking God to meet the needs in my life is that I too have been doing God's work! Since 1978, everything I have been doing has been the work of God! So, if God doesn't meet my need, He doesn't meet His need! I'm not going to hurt over it. He's the one that is going to hurt if the need isn't met. Why? Because it's His work. It is His need.

## God Always Meets His Need

If He tells me to go on ten more television stations, or if He tells me to go do  twenty other things that cost megabucks, it really doesn't make that much difference what the cost is. Why? Because I can't generate it on my own anyway. It is God's project, not mine. If He tells me that He wants me to do it, I don't mind because I know that He is the One Who is going to have to start generating the funds to do the work!

But I've found something out. God always meets His need! If He wants it, He'll get it done! And He will use whoever will be obedient to His voice. So, when God tells you to do something that is impossible in the natural, don't sweat it. It may look impossible.  But that very impossibility is why it *will* work. Faith works in the realm of impossibility. And when you extend yours and start believing that it is possible, your faith will produce the manifestation. When the manifestation arrives, God alone will get the glory because without His intervention you never could have done it!

Do you understand what I'm saying? See, that's faith! That's an attitude of faith in action! So, you make a decision and then you take a step out of the boat. You start walking on the impossible until you reach the goal.

Some ask, "Well, are you expecting to sink?"

"No, because it's His need."

"Well, suppose that He doesn't supply His need?"

"Then He'll go without! And God is not about to do that!"

Now I know this sounds a bit strong, but listen to me. If you want to walk by faith and see the impossible made possible, then you've really got to get this in your heart. Faith only works when you believe! You must truly believe that God is the One giving you the command to come out onto the water. You must truly believe that He will supply you with the means to do what you have to do. Without belief, without faith, you are destined to sink. But with faith you are destined to be a water-walking disciple!

## When You Are Willing to Risk, God Is Able to Move

I believe that the reason why most people haven't seen the great manifestations that we all preach about is because many people never exercise the second part of faith: action! Think about healing and you'll probably be reminded of someone you know who has been "believing" to be healed for years and is still sick.

There is a reason why some people get the physical manifestation of healing and others don't. And it isn't because God is withholding healing from His kids! I believe it is because the second part of Isaiah 53:1 is never preached on. Because of this so many good Christians with good hearts and good intentions never move into the receiving end of healing. They perish for lack of knowledge. See, you may not have a problem with believing that healing is present today. You may not have a problem believing the "report" of the Lord. What you probably have a problem believing is the second question posed in

Isaiah 53:1, **Who hath believed our report?** *and to whom is the arm of the LORD revealed?*

What does that Scripture mean? Well, it asks you two questions, both of which are meant to challenge you to use the power residing within you.

## Whose Report Do You Really Believe?

The first part demonstrates the attitude of faith by asking, *whose report will you believe?* This challenges you to declare, "I will believe the report of the Lord!"

The second part of the Scripture demonstrates the action of faith by asking ...*and to whom is the arm of the LORD revealed?* or, in other words, "who has the power of God — which is capable of producing a physical healing — flowing through them?" That question challenges you to cry out "I do! I am a child of God and His power has been revealed to me! It is flowing through me now!" That is action!

Isaiah 53:1 challenges you with two vital questions whose main purpose is getting you to take a look at what you really believe. It asks what you really believe, not what you heard the preacher talking about last week and not what you say when somebody puts you on the spot. Those questions are there to challenge what you really and truly believe in your own heart. And all of the promises of God — including health! — hinge on your answers to those questions.

So where are you with God? Do you really believe His report? Do you really believe that God's power is capable of saving, healing, prospering and delivering you? Do you believe that, as a born-again Christian, you have the very same power that Jesus had dwelling within you now?

Those are some strong, soul-searching questions, and I'd venture to say that there aren't many Christians in the body of Christ today who can readily answer them in truth. If there were, we wouldn't have so many children of God walking in only a portion of the promises God gave us all.

## Find Out What You Believe

You need to *know* what you believe. And you need to be honest enough to admit it if you find your belief isn't up to par! Don't lie about it and say you really believe these things and then try to work it out in your flesh! If you do, you'll live "believing" instead of "receiving." And believing alone doesn't cut the mustard!

When sickness attacks, "hoping and praying" won't heal you. Faith in God's ability will bring the manifestation of healing into your life.

Think about what Jesus said to those He ministered healing to. He didn't go around saying, "I, Jesus, have made you whole." No, instead He'd say, "Your faith has made you whole." Why did so many people receive so easily? Because Jesus didn't hesitate to stretch out His hand to heal in faith and the people didn't hesitate to reach out and grab hold of the healing! They didn't question Jesus' ability to administer wholeness. How about you?

If you're hesitant, and in your heart you can't say for certain if you really believe His report, then there are things you can do to remedy that!

## You *Can* Believe This! You *Can* Live What You Preach!

Your situation is not hopeless, no matter where you stand today. So don't think that it is. Regardless of whether you've read two Scriptures or two thousand, you can have faith enough to receive! Faith doesn't come by how much you've read; it comes from how much you've heard in your heart! So ask yourself: "How much have I *really* heard? How much has hit home with me?"

If your answers to the questions in Isaiah 53:1 aren't as strong as you'd like them to be, then it's time to start *hearing the Word*. Romans 10:17 (NKJV) says that **faith comes by hearing, and hearing by the Word of God**.

Are you hearing the Word? Are you hearing faith? Unless you're hearing faith, you'll have a hard time mustering up enough of it to see a manifestation.

There is a revelation of health on the inside of you. Your born-again spirit doesn't have a problem with faith, your mind does. So tap into your spirit through study of the healing Scriptures until your mind lines up with what God says. Do it so you can get rid of double-mindedness and worship His awesome power to heal with your spirit, soul and body!

## When Revelation Turns Into Manifestation

"How do I find out the report of the Lord, Brother Jesse?" Good question! The report of the Lord is right there in the Bible. Book after book, chapter after chapter, you can find what God says about everything in life right there in the Book. In fact, He gave you more in that Book than you'll ever need in one lifetime. Why? Because He's too much.

See, when you want to know the report of the Lord, you don't just stop on one Scripture, even though that one is enough to do the job. You keep on studying the Word until you get a revelation of God's outlook on health. When you get a revelation of *to whom the arm of the Lord is revealed,* then revelation turns into manifestation! Then you're out of the wheelchair. Cancer is out of your body. Your blind eyes are open. Your blood pressure goes down. Your flesh is made whole. The report is good, but you must put some action behind it if you want a manifestation.

## Are You Scared of Risk?

Many people have a great attitude of faith. They look up to the Lord for guidance and strength. But they're stumped when it comes to action because they're scared to take a risk. They're worried about the actual outcome of stepping out on faith.

God is *able to do exceeding abundantly above all that we ask or think.* Where's the risk in that?

Do you know what has always amazed me? People who have a dozen problems will come up to the altar for prayer and leave healed of just one problem! The power of God is so strong on them that they're swaying. Their muscles cave in and they can't hold their weight up. They fall to the floor under the anointing of the Lord. And yet they get up with some of the same afflictions they went down with.

As for me, I've made up my mind that God is too much when it comes to healing. I'm not into getting one thing healed and being stuck with a bunch of other sicknesses for the rest of my life! If I'm going to get healed, I want it all! That is like going to a cosmetic surgeon for half a nose job and leaving with one side smooth and straight as an arrow, while the other side is still thick and lumpy! That is the way many people receive healing. Instead of letting the Lord shine in all the facets of their lives, they block Him out of a few and let Him handle only one. How do they block Him out? Well, many times I believe it is because they're scared of taking a risk.

## People Ask Me, "Oh, Jesse. Don't You Ever Get Confused?"

What? Are you crazy? Of course I do! I don't know what I'm doing half the time! I'd say that about ninety-eight percent of the time, I walk up to a pulpit without the foggiest idea of what I'm going to preach on. Does that sound like somebody who's in control of the situation? Does that sound like somebody who knows what's going on? I don't always know what's going on!

Sure, I study the Word. I prepare great sermons that never make it to the pulpit. I love to study the Word. I am an avid reader. My library is filled with volume upon volume of the teachings of great men and women of God. Sometimes I study all through the night. I'm thinking about that sermon all through the day. Then do you know what happens? God throws me a curve ball. I get up to the pulpit and He says, "You're not going to preach that tonight, Jesse." I say, "Well, why'd you let me study all day? I could've been doing something else." He'll answer something like, "*You* needed to hear that, Jesse. It was for *you*. Now, open your Bible and I'll give you what the people need." Man, that'll make you sweat bullets if you don't trust God!

So, I just trust Him. I've got to! I pray. I prepare as if I'm going to preach. And if God leads me differently, then I go with His flow. It's a risk, yeah. But I think it's a greater risk to *not* go with His flow. Lives, the eternal lives of human beings, are at stake. They're staked on my ability to take that risk and flow with God, even if it means I don't always feel comfortable doing it.

## With God, There Are No Real Risks So Surge Into Action!

In the world, people who put their necks on the line stand to lose a lot. But with God, those who risk themselves for the cause of Christ stand to gain too much! That's why you see so many brand-new, born-again Christians getting healed and delivered in one shot. They're like little kids, open-eyed and willing to jump out there and risk everything for God.

And by the same token, that's why you see so many older Christians sick and hurting. They've become so familiar with the Lord, the church and the Bible's teachings that they start resting on their laurels and end up letting doubt and unbelief slither into their hearts. They end up talking more about the report of the Lord but doing less to see it come to pass. Good attitude. Bad action.

Which are you? Will you risk your pride for faith? Or are you talking the talk but not walking the walk? Hey, if God's power is that strong, then get all you can! Revelation will turn into manifestation if you act on it. Stir yourself up and encourage yourself in the Lord!

Even if you have to stare at yourself in the mirror each morning and encourage yourself with Scriptures, it is worth it! All the time you spend talking with Jesus and reminding yourself of His promises will keep your attitude of faith in line. It will help surge you forward into action!

When you get a revelation of your "too much" Father, you will want to experience His "too much" health. Because of your active faith, you won't be able to contain just a healing! As He is healing your body, He'll stuff divine health in you at the same time! All of a sudden you'll find out you're not getting sick any more. What happened? Well, you've spent time with Him and He's blessed you with too much healing! So He has gone over into divine health. When you understand that part, He keeps stuffing you full! And He'll keep stuffing as you use a little until you are *pressed down, shaken together and running over!*

## Chapter Nine
# Sickness Can't Stay in a Person Who Has Too Much!

When you get too much of The God of Too Much, sickness and disease can't stay on your body. Cancer can't cling to you. Diabetes can't cling to you. No disease in the world can stand next to the power of God without being totally obliterated.

Do you know that there aren't any hospitals or doctor's offices in heaven? That's right — they aren't there. And do you know why? Because sickness and disease can't stand in the presence of God! That is why people who have cancer aren't going to get to heaven with it. They won't be able to get through the gates with a sickness. Either they get healed here or they get healed there, but their sickness is not going to make it in heaven! The reason why God wants you to be healed here on earth is so other people can see that healing works.

So, how do you get "too much" of The God of Too Much? By reading "more than enough" of His Word! By continually reminding yourself of what His Word says and by knowing and believing what He said.

## The Devil Doesn't Come to Make You Sick, He Comes to Steal, Kill and Destroy You!

I saw a guy in the Atlanta airport one time. He was standing waiting for the flight just about choking to death. Well, at least he sounded like he was dying. The man had a cold — a nasty, slimy, flu-type of cold. He had this hacking cough and you could hear the snot gurgling in the back of his throat. It was gross. Nobody really wanted to be around him. Including me.

But I figured I'd be nice since everybody else was avoiding him like the plague. So I walked up to him and started a conversation.

"Hey, sounds like you got it bad," I said.

He blew his nose in a handkerchief. It sounded like Niagara Falls. Man, when I think back about it, that guy was plumb full of slime!

"Yeah," he said with a muffled voice, "I tell you what. This is the worst I've ever had."

"Yeah," I agreed with him. "It sounds bad."

Then I figured since I was there I might ought to share a little with him. So I just told him what I thought about the situation.

"Man," I said, "you are the perfect example of the grace and mercy of God."

"What?"

"Yeah. That sickness. It's from the Devil. And the Devil doesn't come to make you sick, sir. He came to kill you. He wanted that stinking cold to beat your brains out, fill up your lungs with fluid until you just suffocate and die. But the great God Jehovah is keeping that trash down. The immune system He created is working to keep death off of you. It ain't Excedrin P.M. It's not Tylenol. It's God! He's stopping the Devil from killing you right now. Think about that the next time you take Excedrin."

It doesn't bother me to tell people what I think. I don't always do it. Sometimes I can be real quiet around people (believe it or not). But that day, I felt like telling that man the truth about sickness — and the truth about God's mercy and grace. He even cares for people who aren't saved. It's just His mercy and grace keeping that sickness from turning into something to destroy, steal and kill.

But just think how much better it is for a Christian. Sickness and disease are not only fought off by the immune system, which is God's grace in our body, they can be fought off in the spiritual realm! How? With God's Word!

## Stir Yourself Up With the Word!

But you don't simply remind yourself of His Word. You stir yourself up! Start quoting those Scriptures to yourself like a preacher, earnestly and fiercely telling your body to line up with the Word! You say things like, "By His stripes I was healed over two thousand years ago and today I'm claiming it over my life!" Search your Sword of the Spirit and find out that...

> I am the LORD that healeth thee.
>
> Exodus 15:26

> And ye shall serve the LORD your God, and he shall bless thy bread, and thy water; and I will take sickness away from the midst of thee.
>
> Exodus 23:25

> And the LORD will take away from thee all sickness...
>
> Deuteronomy 7:15

> O LORD my God, I cried unto thee, and thou hast healed me.
>
> Psalm 30:2

> Why art thou cast down, O my soul? and why art thou disquieted within me? hope thou in God: for I shall yet praise him, who is the health of my countenance, and my God.
>
> Psalm 42:11

> Bless the LORD, O my soul, and forget not all his benefits: Who forgiveth all thine iniquities; who healeth all thy diseases.
>
> Psalm 103:2-3

He sent his word, and healed them, and delivered them from their destructions.

Psalm 107:20

There is that speaketh like the piercings of a sword: but the tongue of the wise is health.

Proverbs 12:18

A merry heart doeth good like a medicine: but a broken spirit drieth the bones.

Proverbs 17:22

But unto you that fear my name shall the Sun of righteousness arise with healing in his wings; and ye shall go forth, and grow up as calves of the stall.

Malachi 4:2

My son, do not forget my teaching, but keep my commands in your heart, for they will prolong  your life many years and bring you prosperity.

Proverbs 3:1-2 NIV

God anointed Jesus of Nazareth with the Holy Ghost and with power: who went about doing good, and healing all that were oppressed of the devil; for God was with Him.

Acts 10:38

But if the Spirit of him that raised up Jesus from the dead dwell in you, he that raised up Christ from the dead shall also quicken your mortal bodies by his Spirit that dwelleth in you.

Romans 8:11

Christ hath redeemed us from the curse of the law, being made a curse for us: for it is written, Cursed is everyone that hangeth on a tree.

Galatians 3:13

Stand up and praise God for His healing benefits! Rejoice over these words from God and begin to use them as your own!

## Your Words Are Powerful!

Your words are powerful! Speak God's Words and you won't go wrong. Proverbs12:18 says that **the tongue of the wise is health!** Why does it say that? Because just a few chapters later in Proverbs18:21 it says **Death and life are in the power of the tongue: and they that love it shall eat the fruit thereof.**

So, choose to speak wisely. Forget stewing over the problem! Start stewing over The Problem Solver, Jesus! And remember that divine health comes from spending time with The Healer.

It's wonderful to be in good health. There is no way I could stay healthy without God in my life! If I just had to go on my family's medical history, I'd already be dead, or at least have come close a few times! Heart attacks, heart disease, cancer and diabetes all run in my family. I can't think of one man down the line, including my father, two brothers and uncles, who hasn't had some sort of heart trouble. As far as I know, I am the only man in my family, besides my favorite uncle (who I happen to look just like) who has *not* had a heart attack before forty years of age. Some have had them as early as their early thirties. And here I am, past forty and healthy! That right there is a testament to the miraculous power of God!

## Pull Yourself Together! Be Whole in Jesus' Name!

You see, I believe that although certain sicknesses run in my family, they don't have a right to run me. Why? Because I believe that God's Word covers *all* sickness and disease, whether it comes from genes or not! His Word is more credible than my family's medical history. Genes aren't more powerful than God! Physical things are not more powerful than spiritual things! God is omnipotent and He knows no limitations. His healing is more than enough and His divine health is too much!

But just because I know that spiritual things are more powerful than physical things doesn't mean that I ignore my physical body. You can't separate spirit, soul and body. All those components together make up *you*. You are a spirit who has a soul that resides within a God-created body. Ignoring one part of you would be disastrous. There is a balance that God wants you to strike within your life so that you use what is in you physically, spiritually and emotionally to live a complete and whole life in Him.

## Ignoring One Part of You Is Unbalanced

In my personal life, I don't totally ignore my body and focus just on my spirit, even though my spirit is the most important part of me. I don't just eat anything my flesh tells me to and go pray about it later. I don't carry a fifty-pound belly and preach about divine health. If I did, I'd be out of balance, with my body pulling on my spirit man, trying to fight a sickness created by a neglected body. The same thing goes for the soul, which is the mind, will and emotions. I don't preach about God's joy and then never renew my mind to the Word and expect two minutes of prayer to wash away a day's worth of trash. People who do that live on an emotional roller-coaster! I don't preach about studying God's Word and praying to Jesus, and then never open my Bible or talk to the Lord! No!

See, ignoring a part of who you are is unbalanced and many times proves to be unhealthy physically. Your body will do what you tell it to do. It will work on what you put in it. What you put in your mind will affect your body. What you put in your spirit will affect your body. What you put in your body will affect your body. So if you're searching for divine health, then you need to pull yourself together. Not just your soul, not just your body. But your spirit, soul and body! As for me, I do what I can in the physical by exercising and eating as healthily as I know how. Sure, sometimes I mess up. That's when I fall on the mercy of God! I fall on His mercy concerning every part of my life.

I also do what I can in the soulish realm — the mind, will and emotions — by renewing my mind to the Word and letting it change my thoughts into His thoughts. I am an anointed vessel of the living God searching out and doing His will! That is not arrogance. It's faith! And thinking like this has kept me healthy. It's the combination of physical and spiritual maintenance that keeps sickness away.

## Don't Back Into the Boiling Pot!

I know the Word works! God, the creator of the universe, said that I could be healthy and I refuse to have anything less than what He said I could have! You know, God has never steered me wrong. His Words have worked for me for years. In fact, the last time I had a physical the doctor told me, "You are the healthiest man I ever placed my hand on."

I said, "Touch me, Doc!"

"Well, what's your success?" he asked me.

"Prayer. You want to pray?"

He went, "Uh, uh, uh."

"Bow your head, Doc." I put my hand on him and prayed for him.

"You know," he said, "in all the years of practice nobody has ever prayed for me. I'm just trying to help people, you know?" He just looked at me and I saw little tears swell up in his eyes. My prayer touched his heart.

"I'll pray for you more than just today, doc." I said, "You can take it to the bank, you got a man who will pray for you. I've got a ministry and we know how to pray!"

"You want some more prayer?" I asked.

"Boy, my son needs it."

"What's his name?"

"Harry."

"Bow your head," I said, "Jesus, get Harry!"

Today, you may not realize the potential that's within your life. You may not understand what you have inside of you. You may tend to walk back and forth between "God is able..." and "you are able...." If you've been vacillating between the two, you have probably already figured out that "you are able" doesn't meet the standard of "God is able."

Before you know it, you're like a Louisiana crawfish. Your hands are always up but you're never going forward. Instead, you're backing up into the boiling pot. Some devil is waiting to grab hold of you and suck the brains right out of your head. Then it's over. Do you understand my parallel?

Don't get sucked into the world's way of separating yourself. You are a whole and complete being — spirit, soul and body — who needs God's help on all accounts. His divine health is available to you. All you have to do is meditate on His Word until it becomes real to you. Get too much God in yourself! When God and His Word is really real to you, you won't have to push and shove yourself to do the things you know you ought to do. You'll want to do what's right! You'll have faith for more than a healing and you won't be satisfied until you're walking in divine health!

Faith always brings a manifestation of healing. Faith means believing that what God said, He will do. If you don't believe Him, then faith can't work to bring about a healing. But if you *do* believe Him, then you will be made whole in Jesus' name! He will not only heal you, He will make a deposit of divine health into your body that will keep on quickening your mortal body as long as you allow it to. You do what you can in the natural and believe God to continue doing what He can in the supernatural!

## Refuse, Resist and Attack Sickness!

I tried being sick. And do you know what? I found out that I didn't like it. I've decided that if stripes were laid on Jesus' back for my health, then I'm going to do all I can to continually make withdrawals of health! God is generous with His healing power and that's why I don't worry about sickness and disease in my life.

When I say something like that people always say, "Well, Brother Jesse, suppose you get sick and die?"

And I reply, "But suppose I don't."

"Well, what are you gonna do if you do?"

"What are you gonna do if I don't?"

I just throw their doubt back at them. I doubt their doubt! They say, "You could get sick."

I say, "I doubt it."

I just don't believe that I will and so, consequently, I don't! That's my faith in action and it's working! In almost twenty years of ministry, I haven't had to call in sick one time!

Sickness isn't fun. Sometimes I wonder why so many Christians receive it so readily. The slightest symptom of sickness could be trying to rear its head and immediately many Christians begin babying themselves. They start complaining and whining. It's almost as if they enjoy the attention sickness gives them. It's almost as if they like talking about how bad they feel. Not me! I hate sickness and I hate to talk about it. It's not only depressing, it's boring! Nobody really wants to hear about it anyway. And who needs the sympathy of people who could care less?

I'll tell you what, if sickness tries to attach itself to my body, I immediately resist it. I don't want the stuff! So I begin attacking it with not only my prayers but my very will. I don't baby that sickness. I don't complain to others and treat myself like a fragile, burdened soul. Why? Because I'm not! I'm strong because the Holy One of Israel lives inside of me! His power flows through my veins and I refuse to let that sickness keep me from doing what God's called me to do!

You won't catch me acting like a weakling if sickness tries to steal my divine health. No way! I'm going to use the power within me to *refuse, resist* and *attack* sickness in the name of Jesus! I use my will. I use my words. I use my actions.

I don't deny sickness, I deny that the sickness has a right to stay on my body! I'm born again. Jesus paid the price for my health. It's as simple as that. Jesus said He did it. So I believe Him. And how dare sickness try and attach itself to me after Jesus already paid the price! That sickness can go back to hell where it came from!

## Actions Speak Even Louder Than Words

On top of using my will and my words, I use actions to defy sickness's power. How do I do that? By preaching on healing and exercising my faith for someone else's healing. I sow seeds of healing by praying and laying hands on others who are sick.

Laying hands on the sick is also a powerful way to administer health to yourself! That's right! You'll feel better and they will too! I believe this is a real truth. I've seen it work within my own life. Because I allow God to use me as a vessel through which He can minister healing to others, I continually reap a harvest of health! This works for me because I understand that the laws of sowing and reaping work. No matter what measure you use, it will be measured back to you the same way. (Matthew 7:2; Mark 4:24.)

Whether you're healthy or not, you should make it a point to pray for others. Praying for the sick is sowing. And sowing prayer for healing can only reproduce a harvest of health on your behalf. You have seeds in your mouth that reproduce after their own kind. That is why speaking well of yourself is so important. Saying that you're healthy, along with practicing a healthy lifestyle and living a life of fellowship with Jesus, produces divine health. And what is divine health but "too much" healing?! That is God. He is too much! He "is able to do exceeding, abundantly above all that you can ask or think, according to the power that worketh in you!"

I speak the Word over others. And the living Word that I speak pumps up my faith even more! See, my mind will shut up and listen to what my mouth has to say. So, if there is doubt attacking my mind, I start talking faith. Then, the doubt has to stop attacking my mind because it's so nosy, it wants to hear what I'm saying. And since faith cometh by hearing and hearing by the Word of God...yeah, you get it! That is a revelation right there if you'll think on it for a while. Use it — it'll help you.

Resist, refuse and attack sickness! Then keep on resisting, refusing and attacking it. Why? You want to be healthy, don't you? Besides, there's nothing that makes the Devil more aggravated than a Christian who refuses to quit! That alone should make you want to do it. Haaaaa! You know I love to get under Old Slew-foot's skin!

So, the next time sickness tries to attach itself to your body, remember this chapter. Come back to it and read through these pages again. Remember Who is living inside you! Remember how powerful you are! Most of all, remember to make a withdrawal of healing from the cross. All that Jesus did on that cross is *too much* for you to use up! So get to it! Refuse! Resist! Attack! Then receive *too much* of His divine health!

## The Bible Is Your Life Book, Your Manual for Living

The subjects in this chapter contain real and practical principles that will work for you, and every bit of it is based on God's infallible Word. See, the Bible is a life book. It's a manual of sorts. Everything you need to live a healthy life is in there. Read it for yourself. Look up what God has to say about your health and see if it doesn't make you shout!

You'd better watch out, though. Too much of God can rub off onto other areas, too, like your marriage, your relationship with your kids and especially in your pocketbook! In much the same way that sickness can't hang around when God is on the scene, lack takes the back door out in the presence of a "too much" God!

# Chapter Ten
# You've Got the Power!

You can't have a testimony until you have a test. You can't have a victory until a battle is fought.

God's "too much" nature is activated by faith. If you've got faith then you've got the ability to change physical things. And that is power! Both in the spiritual and the physical realm, faith produces power! But your power will be tested. Faith is always tested by obstacles in life, so don't get all in a huff when the obstacles come. The more damage you do to the Devil, the more he gets aggravated about it. So what does he do? He tests you with obstacles in the natural realm. He tries to attach sickness to your body, lack to your finances, chaos to your home and confusion to your mind. But you can overcome these things. You can change the test into a *testimony*.

Why? Because you're the one with the power! You're the one with the faith. He's just trying to steal what is already yours, what is residing within your heart. That simple truth can really set you free.

The same is true with prosperity. Do you know that Scripture in Malachi 3:10? It's the one that says **Bring ye all the tithes into the storehouse, that there may be meat in mine house, and prove me now herewith, saith the LORD of hosts, if I will not open you the windows of heaven, and pour you out a blessing, that there shall not be room enough to receive it.** That's the test. I heard one man say once, "Well, what if I give and I don't get anything back?" Well, Malachi 3:10 is the test. You have to test the money, test-i-money! Get it?

It's so easy to point the finger and blame. Many people spend their whole lives doing nothing much but that. They're into fighting people instead of the true author of the trouble, Satan. (Ephesians 6:12.)

The Devil is the author of all that is evil, and that includes poverty *and* sickness.

You may have cancer today. You didn't choose it. Sickness wasn't your choice. But do you know what? The outcome of that test is! You can be healed! You can live in the power of God! Don't get mad at me for saying this! I'm not doing it on my own, I'm only repeating what the Lord says in His Word!

## It's That Spirit!

One time a man asked me, "How'd you get so free?"

I said, "Well, where the Spirit of the Lord is there is liberty. But don't get mad at me for living with it. It's *that* Spirit dwelling within me! It's God, not me!"

I realized after chatting with him for a little bit that he was aggravated with me because I was happy. And he was aggravated with God too. He didn't think God was doing what He was supposed to be doing, and he didn't think He was moving fast enough either.

Well, I shook him up a little because I let him in on the news about God. And if you're struggling with God, I'll let you in on it too: *God is finished.* That's it. He's finished. That is why He sat down. (John 19:30; Hebrews 1:3). He gave you all the power you need and now He's just waiting for you to use it. The Lord shut me down in prayer one time. I thought I was praying good. I had a good prayer session going and man, I mean, I thought I was doing great. Then the Lord said, "Jesse, you're aggravating Me."

I said, "What's the problem?" He said, "Listen to me. Listen, listen, listen! Would you please ask me for something that I have not already given you. You keep asking me for things that are already yours. What is the matter with you? Ask me for something that I haven't given you. You're wasting time, boy. You could have been out there going to get the stuff I've already given you. Now ask me something that I have not given you." He said, "I'm The God of Too Much. I'm able to do exceeding abundantly above all that you ask or think. So, ask for something I *haven't* done!"

## Too Much Inheritance

Joshua 19:8 shows you a God Who is too much. Verse eight begins, **And all the villages that were round about these cities to Baalathbeer** [that's one of those names], **Ramath of** the south. This is the inheritance of the tribe of the children of Simeon according to their families.

Out of the portion of the children of Judah was the inheritance of the children of Simeon: for the part of the children of Judah was *too much* for them...

Now is God a respecter of persons? Does He choose sides? No! So if it was too much for them, why can't it be too much for you?!

> ...therefore the children of Simeon had their inheritance within the inheritance of them.

In other words, Judah had more than just enough! They had way too much! Do you notice how they didn't go and buy a bunch of buildings and just stockpile the inheritance? No! Instead they said, "Man, we got too much. Let's go help out Simeon." Just like Judah, you may be blessed in the city, blessed in the field, blessed going in and blessed going out. (Deuteronomy 28:1-6.) But there may be someone around you that desperately needs to be blessed in the house...much less in the city or in the car or whatever. Do you understand where I'm going with this?

God gave these people too much. But they didn't get greedy with their too much. They were generous! They went out immediately and began to share with those around them.

That is the way we should be, too, not stockpiling our earthly riches and helping no one but ourselves, but sharing our abundance with others! Blessing the families of the earth is God's way! (Genesis 12:3.) It is one of the reasons why He gives too much! God doesn't mind you having things, as long as things don't have you!

## Do You Say What God Says
## Or Do You Rely on Past Experiences for Truth?

I preach in all types of churches. Many times I hear doctrines that I do not agree with. And I have an opportunity many times to address those doctrines. I've had some of my friends say, "Jesse, why don't you nail it? You've got an opportunity to hit this thing right in the head!" And sometimes I want to. I'm just as human as anybody.

If I hear someone saying something stupid about my God I want to slap them and say, "What's the matter with you?!" If I flip the channels and find a preacher saying something stupid on the television I want to go through the tube and holler, "Shut up!" I wonder how many people have found themselves feeling the same way.

Most of the time, I find that preachers who veer off from the Word of God get there by relying on past experiences. That is where you get people saying things like, "Don't seek after faith," or "God doesn't heal everybody, you know. Sometimes He does and then sometimes He doesn't," and "Don't get crazy with that faith thing. Suppose it doesn't work. Then you'll look like a fool."

How do they back up those doctrines? They say things like, "I know Sister So-and-So who was a saint of God, who loved the Lord with all her heart, who had more faith than anybody in the room and yet even she died." See, that is a doctrine based upon an earthly experience.

Well, I don't doubt that Sister So-and-So was a saint of God, who loved the Lord with all her heart. I don't doubt that she had more faith than anyone in the room. What I pose is that maybe if the people around her would have had a little bit more faith she would have lived. Maybe she would have lived if everyone around her hadn't been saying, "Oh, she looks so bad. This sickness is a killer, you know. We'll hope and pray, but you never know what God is going to do. He may want to take her on home...blah, blah, blah..." Her faith mixed with the strong faith of others might have gotten it to work!

## Don't Blame God

Besides, you don't know what's in somebody's heart. They could be going to church for forty years and have faith to believe God for everyone else to be healed. But when it comes to them, they may have become weary. They might not have the strength to believe for themselves, and they might need strong faith from those around them in order to receive the healing. Sometimes, whether we want to believe it or not, people don't want to fight the good fight of faith. Sometimes, there are people who would rather die and go home to be with Jesus than fight the sickness Satan attacked them with. And hey, whether we like it or not, it's their choice. The will to live and not die must be burning in their hearts if they are going to receive the power of healing in their lives.

This is a hard situation because many times the family really does have faith to believe for the healing. The person who is sick has the faith to believe for a healing. Everyone prays. Then, if the person dies, often it shakes the family so much that they begin to denounce faith and become somewhat angry at God. They begin to reassess what they believe about God. They wouldn't think of putting the blame for the death on anyone but God. After all, they did everything they could, right? Well, yes, they might have done everything they *knew* to do. But as much as it hurts to say it, God still isn't the one to blame.

God always has his hand out to heal. He never lies. He's able to heal. *God is able to do exceeding abundantly above all that we ask or think,* **according to the power that worketh in us.** So why did that person die? *According to the power that worketh in us.* The family had the power. The sick person had the power. But was it working? Did the manifestation of healing present itself? No. Why wasn't it working? Ahhh, now that's the question. Why wasn't the power of God that is able to do exceeding abundantly above all that we ask or think working in this situation? What went wrong?

These are good questions to ask yourself if a situation like this comes up in your life. Not so that you can pin the blame on somebody, but so that you can understand that sometimes we as humans fall short of the Glory of God. We don't always know how to use the power that worketh in us. Through ignorance of the Word, many people perish.

Some perish because in their hearts they believe more in the doctor's report than in the report of the Lord. Some perish because those around them drown their faith through anti-faith speaking and acting. (These people must war against both sickness and doubt, and sometimes they are too weary to overcome.) Some perish because they are totally dependent on another person's faith.

And for some, well, it goes even deeper. They know what faith is. They know how to use that faith for a healing. But inside, there is something deeper that draws them. That makes them agree in faith with their lips but disagree in their heart. Most of the time this is the person who knows God. This is the person who has reached a state of peace with God. And they've finally reached the point in their life where they aren't afraid to meet Him face to face. In fact, they are the ones who are willing to accept defeat in order to do just that.

## My Experience Doesn't Change God's Word

Listen, I know what I'm talking about here. I've been in this situation myself. My mother died on Easter Sunday when she was only forty-nine years old. She was the single most powerful spirit-filled Christian woman I've known. She was a strong Bible-believing woman. She believed for a healing of cancer for herself and was healed of it...twice!

That day in the hospital, she didn't have to die. Between my daddy and me, we had enough faith to keep her alive. In fact, we did just that for a while. But do you know what? My mama wanted to go home to be with Jesus. She was tired of fighting. She no longer had a burning will to live. And that was the clincher. Sure, she didn't really want to die sick. But since it was happening, she made a decision in her heart that going home to be with Jesus was better than hanging out on the earth.

We fought her decision tooth and nail. My daddy wanted his wife. My family and I wanted our mama. We wanted her to stay in Louisiana more than anything else.

Mama let us pray over her. She even agreed in prayer with us. But she was an honest woman, and she couldn't let us keep praying when her heart was hiding a secret that fought our prayers at every turn. And eventually she told us point blank and bluntly, "Leave me alone! Let me go!" We hollered, "No! You're going to be healed!" She was such a strong-willed woman. It was hurtful and irritating to see her letting her life slip away. She had the power to fight! I knew this from first-hand experience. Sick or not, this woman had the strength of God in her. Yet, she was slipping.

Angry, I left the room. My eyes hot with tears and my heart thumping with adrenaline, I flew into a torrent of angry prayers to God. I was mad at my mama. I was mad at the situation. I was mad at God, too. Wasn't He listening? With fierce prayers and determination to see my mother healed, I started talking to God. "What is going on here?! I'm praying! Dad's praying! Why isn't she healed? You cannot allow death to defeat me, God. You made a covenant with me through Jesus' blood! And that covenant says by His stripes we were healed! Where is that healing? If you break this covenant with me, you'll have to cease to be God! You must keep covenant with me. You must obey your Word!" I was honest with God. He knew how I felt, so what was the point in hiding it. I was confused. I was hurt. I didn't know what else to do.

That is when God spoke up, "Jesse, I have a covenant with you, yes. But I have one with your mother as well. You are praying for her healing. She is praying in her heart for Me to take her home. Now, I will obey My Word. But you and your daddy are battling your mother's will. And it is her life at stake. You have Me in a hard place, Jesse. Someone has got to give in. Get yourselves together and tell Me what I am to do!"

I flew back into my mother's room. I looked at her. She was the most hard-headed woman in the world. You know, my mama never listened to anybody. She did what she wanted to do most of the time. And she always said that when all her family was saved, she'd go home to be with Jesus. Well, we all had come in and here she was, obeying her own negative words of death. It made me mad. How stupid! Only forty-nine years old! But I knew I couldn't fight her forever. She had more staying power than all of us. That we knew.

So, I talked to Dad. And with hearts wrenched with anger and sorrow, we released my mama. We let her have her way. And do you know what? The second we agreed to let her go, she stopped breathing. The sound of her heart monitor went flat. I heard her breathe her last slow, raspy breath. And then...she was gone.

Immediately my sister, who was in the waiting room, heard mama's voice, "I'm free, Debra! I'm free!"

Debra didn't know what happened. She came running in the room. Mama had just gone home to be with Jesus. It was Easter Sunday morning, 1982. It was just like Mama to go out dramatically. Just like her to die on the day all of heaven would be having a party.

See, I believe God's Word. I believe His Word over man's experience. I could say that God didn't heal my mother. But that would be a lie. God did heal her. She just didn't accept the healing.

God cannot and will not lie. Stripes were laid on Jesus' back for healing and health for all. But they are received through faith. I know this because Jesus said it over and over throughout the Gospels of Matthew, Mark, Luke and John. Faith isn't lip service, it's heart service. Although the words of your mouth are powerful, they don't mean much if they aren't coming from the heart. I believe that it's not what you pray with your mouth so much as what you believe in your heart that counts when it comes to faith.

My mama agreed with our prayers, but it was lip service. She was honest with us in the end. Some people aren't honest about what's in their hearts; they're afraid of what people will think. But I'm glad that Mama let us know what she really wanted. I thought she was being stupid, acting like a crazy woman. I still think she should have tapped into that healing power and saved herself from death. But I couldn't break her will with my own. She wanted to go.

I wonder how many have died because they were surrounded by unbelieving, negative-speaking people who sowed unbelief in a situation that requires pure belief? How many were too weary to fight their doubt and the sickness? How many Christians pray in lip service, while their hearts contradict those fervent prayers? How many others have been on their deathbed and, like my mother, would rather die and go to heaven than fight the fight of faith? How many die not telling their loved ones that they are finished fighting, ready to go home?

There are all sorts of issues in situations such as these. But not one of those issues changes the Word of God. His Word is eternal. It is Truth. It is Life. It is all these things to those who receive it.

## We Aren't Pawns on God's Chessboard

Nobody seems to want to hear this kind of thing because it shifts responsibility from God to man. Sadly, very few people are willing to take up their responsibility with gladness. They'd rather blame God than ever take a good, harsh look at themselves. God forbid it's something they're doing! They'd rather pretend to be God's chess pawns, pretend that He is moving them through life like inanimate objects.

But God never intended for people to be inanimate objects. He created man with a will and gave Him the responsibility of faith! God did His part when He sent Jesus to the cross. And like I said before, if shifting the responsibility to someone regarding faith is cruel, then Jesus was the cruelest man alive.

It is easier to blame God, whom you can't see, than to chalk the experience up to our own disregard or lack of faith. But don't start pointing the finger at whoever you think is lacking. Don't ever blame God and don't judge your family and friends. You may share what you know about faith and about the power of words and the power of knowing your own heart. But never, ever criticize and blame. It isn't God's way and it'll only bring strife and condemnation.

Instead, take a look inside of yourself first. Find out what is in your heart. Listen to what is coming out of your mouth. Get the log out of your own eye first before you try and pick a splinter out of somebody else's. (Matthew 7:3-5.)

## Beware of Those Who Flip-flop!

As for me, I refuse to be moved by religious experiences because I know that they are not concrete truths and they'll not give me life. Instead, I try to focus on what God said instead of what experience has said.

Sure, I know that Satan will be slick about it. I know he'll get a man or woman whom I esteem highly in the faith to try and steer me off the Word. The Devil will often use someone you respect and honor, whose opinion you will hear and adopt as your own, to steer you off the Word. Remember that the next time you hear a preacher or someone you esteem highly say something like, "Don't do that. I tried it and it doesn't work." Just because he tried it and it didn't work doesn't mean that it is not true!

That's like saying, "Don't get on that track and try to run five miles! I tried it and it didn't work!" Well, yeah, maybe you did try to get on that track and run five miles. And maybe you passed out trying. But it doesn't mean it can't be done. With the right training, anyone can do it. Training is the key.

Most people think, "Well, if it didn't work for that guy, how is it ever going to work for *me?*" And they back away from the true concept of God — the God that is not enough, He's too much. Before you know it, entire ministries are built on someone else's religious experience.

Of course there will be some things in life that you just don't understand. You don't know what went wrong and you can't understand why. But don't immediately change your opinion of the Bible because of it. Don't discount God because of earthly experience. Your experience is not higher than God's Word. And if you try and make a new religion out of your cross-breed of God's Word and man's experience, you will end up sad and confused. It is miserable to flip-flop between what God said and what experience has said. It is no way to live, I'll tell you that much!

God does not change. Beware of people and preachers who do. Guard your ears and make sure you're not filling your heart with man's experience. It is your responsibility to make sure you're filling your heart with God's Word. And He is saying the same thing today that He did in Bible days. He hasn't changed ever, and He isn't going to start now. **Jesus Christ the same yesterday, and to day, and for ever** (Hebrews 13:8).

## "I Just Don't Understand, God!"

If you're confused about a situation, don't turn around and start spouting off all your confusion to those around you. You may cause someone to stumble if you do. Instead, get alone with God and seek His face concerning your own part in the matter. Then pray for all the others involved. You may not know the hearts of the others, but you can sure make yourself aware of your own heart. And God will show you if you need to rectify something concerning yourself. He'll do it in love and He'll shower you in peace about the matter.

It isn't your responsibility to change the heart of someone else. You'll never know them well enough to do it anyway. It is God who changes the hearts of men and women. He looks into their souls and He will do the same for you as you open yourself up to Him. He will get in that heart of yours and mend, straighten and clean up all the parts that you allow Him to!

If you'll open up and be honest with Him, He'll pour in His too much! But you, not God, set the gauge for how much you're going to get. He's willing to overload you with salvation, health, prosperity, peace and joy! It's you who determine whether you'll take any of it. It is you who determine how much of His "too much" you're going to take.

## When It Comes to Jesus, I'm Not Changing!

Throughout my years of ministry, I've had many people tell me, "Jesse, you haven't changed. You still preach the same stuff as when you first started." I consider that a high compliment. Why? Because God hasn't changed, and, since I'm preaching His Word, it means I haven't veered off the track into man's experiences! Hallelujah!

Of course, in my flesh I'd probably appreciate it if He *would* change. Just a little. Maybe one day He would decide, "Ahhh, forget about this mercy stuff. I'm going to burn up everyone alive who's messed with Jesse." Yeah! Sometimes I think that would be great. Maybe you've caught yourself thinking that too!

Sometimes you just have someone who is a thorn in your flesh. Well, more like a complete bush! All bristly and sharp, they're willing to cut your guts out the minute you turn your back! It is that type of fellow Christian that you pray for judgement on! "Ohhhh, Lord. Kill 'em, God. Do what You have to do, but hurt 'em a little bit, God!" You want to get in the flesh a little and start making up prophecy, saying something like, "You've been weighed in the balances and found wanting, you honky devil from hell. You're gonna get busted between the eyes and I'm gonna use Jesse to do it, thus saith the Lord!" Wow, wouldn't that be something if God really said that?! Of course He wouldn't, though — He doesn't change.

How many Scriptures are there that you wish you could just rip out of the Bible? In fact, I can think of one right now that sometimes I wish God would have cut off midway through the verse. Hebrews 10:30 (NKJV) could have been my favorite Scripture. It's the one that goes **vengeance is Mine, I will repay, says the Lord.** Sometimes my flesh feels He should have left *says the Lord* off. That way I could just claim *vengeance is mine!* Wouldn't that be great? You could slap somebody silly and feel good about it!

I'm sure everybody feels that way, but I sometimes feel like it's worse for preachers. If you're a preacher, those thorn-bush people can be really bad. You're supposed to be the example of love, but sometimes, well, you just would rather tell them where to go (i.e. hell) and repent later. Hey, I'm being honest.

I imagine if you're a pastor it could be worse. There are just some people you would rather not have come to your church. Don't lie about it! You end up going up to them and saying, "Listen, sister. I know a good brother that needs you down the road. He pastors such-and-such church down the way and he really could use a dear soul like yourself." And that good brother down the way says, "I can't believe you sent that crazy fool down here!"

One time I asked God about all those crazy Christians. I said, "Lord, you got some crazy people here! I may be one of them, but you got some fruitcakes amongst us. God, you've got some bad — and I mean *bad* — kids! I just don't know if they're even saved!"

And do you know what He said to me? He said, "Jesse. They're still my kids. They're just some of my bad kids." He said, "You ought to know about that. You were a bad kid, too."

He was right. I was a bad kid. I was always an entrepreneur. Me and my brother hated each other until we became men. It seemed like he'd beat me up once a day. But I did my part, too. One time I sold his clothes. I sold his clothes! I wiped him out in a day. Then I sold his toys. I went down the street and I came back with about eight dollars. We were poor and his junk wasn't worth much.

Wayne said, "Mama, I ain't got no clothes. Jesse sold all my clothes. He sold my toys, too!"

I thought to myself, "You mess with me and I'll sell you. I know somebody who wants you!"

Boy, Mama would get so mad at us! She'd make us repent. But she wouldn't make us repent by saying we're sorry. She'd do something much, much worse.

"What's the matter with you boys?" Mama would cry. "You're supposed to luuuuuvve your brother. Now, kiss your brother and make up." Augggh! I hated it!

I'd say, "I ain't kissing him!" Boy, we'd start an argument! "I hate you," I'd bark at him. He wasn't too fond of me either.

Mama would say, "You kiss your brother and you act like you like it, Jesse!" So both of us would clinch up and go as fast as we could. *Smack!* A kiss planted on the cheek as hard as we could. We were hoping to make a bruise with that kiss.

"Do it again! Hug your brother and kiss your brother!"

Augggh! We'd get close. I'd reach out there to hug him and simultaneously we'd start pinching each other on the back.

See, Mama made us use faith and action. But it produced power, which was  tested by an obstacle...my brother! Ahhhh! It all ties in, you see!

## Chapter Eleven
# Taking Off the Limits

I've got a pretty good imagination. When I was a kid my mom said I could play with a little Matchbox car all day. I wouldn't have to leave the room to make a car trip from the East Coast to the West Coast! I had a blast!

Today I still have a good imagination. And I don't believe God gave it to me for nothing. He isn't scared of me reading Ephesians 3:20 and using my imagination.

He doesn't get His feathers ruffled when I turn to that part in the Bible and proclaim it out loud to myself: **Now unto him that is able to do exceeding abundantly above all that we ask or think, according to the power that worketh in us, Unto him be glory in the church by Christ Jesus throughout all ages, world without end. Amen!** See, I believe 2 Timothy 3:16 when it says **all scripture is given by inspiration of God, and is profitable for doctrine, for reproof, for correction, for instruction in righteousness.**

Ephesians 3:20 is as much for me today as it was for the church at Ephesus two thousand years ago!

Although most of the church world frets and worries over people believing and receiving Ephesians 3:20, God doesn't! He did it on purpose! He knew you were going to read it. So He wanted to make sure you knew that He was too much! He said He's able to do *all* that you ask or think. And He meant what He said!

## God Doesn't Limit Man; Man Limits God

What is limiting you today? Is it a lack of faith?

Maybe. Lack of action? Possibly. But before you can even start dealing with that, let me offer you one other option. I propose that what is really limiting you is *your thinking*. Are you bound up with poverty of thought? Have you been told all your life that prosperity isn't for you? Maybe you've been told that you'll be poor your whole life.

Man puts the limits on prosperity. Not God. Because with God, there is no limit. God has created us and given us limitless possibilities in this life. And He's given each of us an imagination in which to think extraordinarily, not ordinarily!

So maybe you haven't been able to get through with your faith because your thinking has contradicted your spirit. Maybe it's because you haven't allowed yourself to truly believe like a child; to have imagination like a child; to have faith like a child.

You see, there is no limit to our asking, only to our thinking. It is poverty of thought that keeps poverty in our life. Small thoughts produce small deeds.

If you pastor a small church, don't be embarrassed if it's small. It isn't a shame to be small. But it is a shame to *stay* small. A growing church means that people are receiving Christ and their lives are being turned around for the better.

Quit doing the best you can. The best *you* can doesn't work. God is able to get that church growing! He's able to get your life going! Quit trying to do His job. Don't take the burden of growth in any area of your life onto yourself. Seek God and love Him. You will grow.

**Now unto him that is able to do exceeding abundantly above all that we ask or think,** *according to the power that worketh in us*. God's part is everything except the last eight words of Ephesians 3:20. You don't have to try and do the exceeding abundantly above great things. Your part is the last eight words...**according to the power that worketh in us.** That's the only part you have to make this thing work. It's faith. And it's where the power is!

From where does the power come? From God? Yes. But it works through the God-created soul of man; his mind, will and emotions. I believe it begins in the mind, and that power is enforced by the stern will and creative emotions God has placed within each of us.

Our thinking must be tuned into God. You and I both know that a double-minded man is unstable in all his ways. (James 1:8.) You can't serve God and mammon. (Matthew 6:24; Luke 16:13.) You can't flip-flop between "I believe" and "Well, I don't know." That just doesn't work with God...or in any other facet of life, for that matter!

If you look at Deuteronomy 28, you'll see that God doesn't just say, "I'll bless you." He says, "I'll bless you coming in...going out...in the field...in the city...." He tells you not only that, "I'm gonna bless you!" but specifically, "I'm gonna bless you in these places...!"

God doesn't have an empty mind. He isn't limited to what you can do. So you don't have to be limited in what you ask or think. Just as long as it doesn't contradict God's Word, you can ask what you will and He will do it for you. (John 15:7.)

## You Can't Exhaust God!

God is too much. You can't exhaust His promises. When they fall from His lips they become prophetic utterances to His children. They immediately become prophecies that will come to pass if we follow His lead! You can take it to the bank. If God says He is able, then He is able! And He moves according to the power that is working in us.

When you tap into His resources through faith and sowing, God will start blessing you financially. You'd better get some baskets! You'd better get some trucks! I love what another one of my minister friends says about prosperity. When you get into that perfect will of God, my friend says, God will "increase your increase." Now, that's increase!

Have you asked God for physical things? Sure, most of us have. Yet why is it that the church world seems so bent on your *not* asking for physical things? Have you ever wondered why they seem so quick to tell you to give and so reluctant to tell you to receive a harvest? And this doesn't just go on in traditional churches; it happens in fundamental spirit-filled churches as well. They actually condemn "giving to get" and make you feel so guilty for receiving a harvest that many people just let their prosperity seeds rot in the ground. I'll say it again: *there is nothing wrong with having things, so long as things don't have you.*

God is able to do exceeding abundantly above all you ask or think...so let your mind soar. You can never ask too much. You can never think too much. Why? Because you'll never get beyond God's ability. He's limitless!

So what can you see? What can you imagine doing in this life for Him? Can you throw off the old thinking that keeps your feet on the ground and expand your mind into the heavens? What is the greatest thing you can think of asking Him for?

## Don't Get Mad at Me for Believing God's Word!

Of course, I'm not talking about obsessing over houses, cars, clothes or jewelry. I won't even deal with it because you and I both know that obsessing over prosperity is of the flesh. We all know in our hearts that it is wrong. The only thing you should be obsessing over is Jesus! But if you do that, you'll end up with physical things! So, there you go! You can't get around that prosperity thing. It's just too much!

If I delight myself therefore in Him, He gives me the desires of my heart. (Psalm 37:4, author's paraphrase.)

Don't get mad at me for repeating the Scripture. Don't get aggravated with me for receiving that promise into my life. I haven't said it, I've just read it!

Pray like the psalmist David: **The LORD is my shepherd, I shall not want** (Psalm 23:1).

Shall not want? That is a hefty promise! But David didn't say you would not, he said you shall not! You'll never get to the point of "would not" because you *shall not!*

## Patience Is a Key to Receiving

If you let patience have its perfect work, you'll be perfect and entire, wanting nothing. (James 1:4.) And don't let that word "perfect" throw you. Perfect is simply King James-era language for mature. In other words, if you allow patience to develop to a mature state in your life — by keeping faith operating in your life — then you will find that you will literally want nothing. Why would you want nothing? Because you have everything you need in the Lord Jesus Christ! Patience is the key to receiving! And God always takes care of His kids when they have their eyes on His Son, Jesus.

Remember, you'll be practicing patience (defined in Strong's Concordance as "cheerful endurance" or "constancy.")[1] You'll be putting God first, and that can only lead to one thing: **Seek ye first the kingdom of God, and his righteousness; and all these things shall be added unto you** (Matthew 6:33).

So, you'll want nothing...but it'll only be because you already have all you want in Jesus!

---

[1] James Strong, "Greek Dictionary of the New Testament," *The New Strong's Exhaustive Concordance of the Bible* (Nashville: Thomas Nelson Publishers, 1984), p. 74, #5281.

## Are You Naked? Get Dressed!
## Put On the Full Armor of God!

There are people walking around naked! Buck naked! Don't look around, look down! Is it you? Are you naked? You know, God has given us a full suit of clothes; a full armor to wear as we daily fight the good fight of faith. Did you notice that I said *good* fight? Faith is a good fight! (1 Timothy 6:12.)

You aren't one of those people who are just walking around with a helmet, are you? You aren't one of those who don't like to be burdened down with a full suit of armor, are you?

They're out there, you know. Naked Christians with their helmets on cock-eyed and struggling to see what's going on out there. Some of them just have a helmet and one shoe. Others have a helmet and a breastplate, but their loins...well, uh, let's just say they aren't girded. Then there are those who have that helmet latched on tight and they're swinging their Sword of the Spirit at anything that moves. They're looking to cut something good! They just can't seem to understand why or how they got so many fiery darts stuck in their rear end!

You don't have to be a rocket scientist to figure out that if you've got a dart stuck in your behind, there's a battle going on. If you're looking down and all you see is the color of your bare flesh, then I've got something to tell you. You're naked. Don't you think it's time you put some clothes on?

Put on the whole armor of God! See how it feels to be totally dressed! Hello? A battle is raging as we speak! And if you don't want to be slain by fiery darts and die partially clothed or buck-naked in a helmet, it's time you suit up.

So, come on! Secure that helmet of salvation! Latch on that breastplate of righteousness! Gird up those loins with

Truth! (Not adultery and fornication. Truth!) Slide your feet into the shoes of the preparation of the Gospel of peace. (Peace, not gossip and strife!) Then lock your arm through the shield of faith and grab that Sword of the Spirit! Wow! That armor is just too much!

Go ahead, look in the mirror and tell me what you see. God?! Yeah, it's His armor! You look like Him! And do you know what? The Devil can't even tell it's you when you're wearing that armor! He thinks you are God! Stupid Devil. He's such an idiot.

But as long as he thinks you are God, you might as well use it to your advantage. Go ahead and slice that fool down to size with your Sword of the Spirit. Careful not to cut your brother! Oh, yeah? The Devil is shooting darts at you? Throw up that shield of faith and laugh! He can't hurt you with his puny darts. You've got the shield of faith that is able to quench all the fiery darts. (Ephesians 6:16.)

The only way the Devil can beat you is if you're naked, or partially suited. Forget to lock on your breastplate of righteousness and he can shoot you in the chest. Forget to wear your shoes and he can shoot you in the oot. Forget to gird up your loins and you're in for some pain. Forget to equip yourself with the Sword of the Spirit and, well...you've got nothing to fight with.

The armor of God isn't enough, it's too much. It really is more than you need. It's bigger than you need. It's stronger than you need. You can't damage it. The Sword of the Spirit holds more power to fight the enemy than you can use up in your entire lifetime. Your helmet of salvation latches on so tight, it literally becomes part of you. You are the only one that can remove it. Each piece of God's indestructible armor could rightly be called "too much."

## Your Only Enemy Is Satan

You know that armor isn't there because you are at war with other people. It's available to you so that you can be safe from the enemy, all principalities and powers of the air. Yes, the Devil. You live in love and peace with people. You live in war with the evil spirit that moves upon people and situations. Recognize that and you'll have most of the problems with people beat. But somehow we forget about that and want to bust a few people we know! Hey, I'm with you. I know a few people that make me feel like I wanna get out my boxing gloves! I'd love to rip out the page in the Bible, Matthew 5:44, that says **But I say unto you, Love your enemies, bless them that curse you, do good to them that hate you, and pray for them which despitefully use you, and persecute you....** Ugh! Pray for them? I'd rather shoot them!

But that is the flesh nature. You and I know it. This is hard sometimes. You've got to remind yourself in prayer that these people are not devils from hell. They may act like devils from hell. They may sound like devils from hell. They may even look like devils from hell! But they are not devils from hell. They're run by them, they're influenced by them, but still they are not them.

Believe it or not, praying for your enemies actually helps. Yeah, I know you want to curse them. But bite your lip and pray for them instead. It's the only way to stop bitterness and unforgiveness from taking root in your heart. Sure, cursing them comes into your head. Just cast those thoughts down in the name of Jesus and don't let them take root in your heart. "How do I do that?" you say. Speak up. Say, with your mouth, good things. Say forgiving things. Repent for thinking that way, out loud. Your doubting mind will shut up long enough to hear what your mouth is saying. Speak the Word over them and watch those thoughts melt into the love of God. He can help you love them, you know. But you'll have to put forth some effort in the process.

## God Doesn't Make Exceptions

There are some basic rules to Christianity. One of them, the most important of them, is Jesus. You'd never think of trying to lead someone else to the Lord without mentioning Jesus, would you? Of course you wouldn't! The Scripture plainly says, quoting Jesus in John 14:6, **I am the way, the truth, and the life: no man cometh unto the Father, but by me.** This is the number-one rule of Christianity. No Jesus, no heaven. Plain and simple.

If God made an exception and let someone into heaven who didn't first call on the name of Jesus, then you could rightly call God prejudiced for giving eternal life to one and not the other on the basis of whim. If God did that, He would be disregarding His Word, and from then on you would not be able to trust Him to keep His promises.

But God is not prejudiced and His Word is unchangeable. He won't break a promise and He cannot lie. **God is not a man, that he should lie; neither is the son of man, that he**

**should repent: hath he said, and shall he not do it? or hath he spoken, and shall he not make it good?** (Numbers 23:19).

What God has said is exactly what He will do. If God said you have to receive Jesus before you can get to Him, then guess what? You have to receive Jesus before you can get to God! It's that simple and there aren't any exceptions.

## Hearing It. Receiving It. Believing It. That's Faith!

Salvation seems easy enough to receive, doesn't it? Sometimes I wonder why it is so easy for people to believe that God doesn't make exceptions when it comes to salvation, and yet it's so difficult for them to believe He doesn't make exceptions when it comes to physical healing and earthly prosperity. But you know, it's true. He is the same way with all those things. By *faith* you receive salvation. By *faith* you receive healing. By *faith* you receive earthly prosperity.

And yet the faith needed to obtain all these things begins first in your ears (hearing) and then moves into your mind (receiving) and then into your heart (believing).

If you think about when you got saved, you'll notice that first somebody had to tell you about Jesus. Then, as you listened, your mind began to receive the message they were telling you. You began to receive what they were telling you was true. Then you turned to God and opened your heart directly to Him by expressing your new belief in His Son. You showed God you needed Him. You were sincere. And you had faith that He was listening to the words that you spoke from your heart.

Consequently, you were saved.

The mind, then, has a lot to do with salvation. You can't disregard the mind. It is where information is processed and it is the link to your heart. It is the link to your faith. I'm going to say it again: you hear with your ears, you receive with your mind, you believe with your heart!

That means that if your mind is empty — if your mind does not receive the message as important or vital — then God is limited as to what He can do for you. If your will is idle and you are not sincerely opening your mind to the message, then God is limited as to how He can move on your behalf.

Why? Because it is through the faith and prayers of His children that God moves within the earth. And faith comes from the heart. Yet before it gets to the heart it must go through the ears and mind.

So if you are hearing with your ears but not receiving it with your mind, which is doubting, then how are you ever going to start believing? How is the Word ever going to get into your heart, where you believe? And if you're hearing the Word but not believing it's really true, then how do you expect to have the faith needed to bring about a manifestation? These steps are what you might call the laws of faith. You've got to trust in them if you want to see results. Faith works. There's no doubt about it. So let's look to the Bible and find out how it worked in the lives of others. Read on to chapter 12 and find out how faith makes things happen!

# Chapter Twelve
## Faith Makes Things Happen!

There are so many Scriptures that show us that when we believe (trust in, rely on and have faith in) God, things happen! Prayers are answered! Manifestations of His power come to full light! These are just a few of the Scriptures that prove what happens when a person truly believes...what happens when they have faith in God.

Taken from the New International Version and New King James Version, each of these Scriptures relates to a different person who believed God during a different time. Although they are thousands of years old, these few scenarios, I believe, will help to illustrate my point about faith in God. Let's begin in the Old Testament:

**Abraham believed the LORD, and he credited it to him as righteousness** (Genesis 15:6, NIV). God saw that Abraham *believed* Him. This was so moving to God that He credited Abraham with righteousness, which allowed him to speak with God! A pretty heavy credit, seeing that Jesus hadn't yet died to make all of us righteous!

**"Now give me this hill country that the Lord promised me that day. You yourself heard then that the Anakites were there and their cities were large and fortified, but, the Lord helping me, I will drive them out just as he said"** (Joshua 14:12, NIV). Caleb *believed* the Lord, and, after spying out the land, he had a good report. Because of Caleb's faith in God, God caused him to inherit the very land he had reported on. Why was he blessed with prosperity of land? Well, the Scripture plainly says it was because he wholly followed the Lord God of Israel! Caleb's faith brought him prosperity!

**"The Lord who delivered me from the paw of the lion and the paw of the bear will deliver me from the hand of this Philistine"** (1 Samuel 17:37, NIV). David *believed* God! He had faith that God would deliver victory no matter how dire the circumstances looked! Because of faith, a giant lost his head and David gained a throne! David's faith brought him victory in battle and authority in his homeland!

**"Be strong and courageous. Do not be afraid or discouraged because of the king of Assyria and the vast army with him, for there is a greater power with us than with him"** (2 Chronicles 32:7, NIV). During wartime, Hezekiah *believed* that God was a greater power. He believed God was on his side. And what did God do in return? He sent an angel to defeat the enemy! God saved Hezekiah and the inhabitants of Jerusalem from the hand of not only that enemy but, the Scripture says, of all others. It also says that God guided them on every side! Not only that, but a few lines down you find out that Hezekiah had very great riches and honor and that God had given him very much property. Those are some of the things God does for people who believe Him!

**"If we are thrown into the blazing furnace, the God we serve is able to save us from it, and he will rescue us from your hand, O king"** (Daniel 3:17, NIV). Shadrach, Meshach and Abednego had *faith* in God! They believed that God would rescue them and He did just that! All three were thrown in the fire, but God sent a fourth man into the flame to rescue them from fiery execution. And the Bible says they got out without even burning their hair! On top of that, their faith in God converted the very king who sent them into the flames! Just a few lines down (Daniel 3:30, NIV) you can read: **Then the king promoted Shadrach, Meshach and Abednego in the province of Babylon.** Their faith brought them deliverance from death and promotion in life!

Now let's read together from the New Testament. And since the New Testament is so straightforward concerning faith, I'm not going to elaborate on each Scripture. These Scriptures are not so much stories of faith as they are direct words of encouragement and enlightenment, each of which teaches us more about what faith is and what faith does. They need no elaboration; they stand alone.

Read them to yourself. Do it out loud if you can. I want you to hear them with your ears and then receive them in your mind so you can have the ability to believe them in your heart. Read on:

> *Now faith is* the substance of things hoped for, the evidence of things not seen.
>
> **Hebrews 11:1, NKJV**

By *faith we understand* that the universe was formed at God's command, so that what is seen was not made out of what was visible.

Hebrews 11:3, NIV

By *faith* Enoch was taken from this life, so that he did not experience death; he could not be found, because God had taken him away. For before he was taken, he was commended as one who *pleased God.*

Hebrews 11:5, NIV

And without faith it is impossible to please God, because anyone who comes to him must believe that he exists and that he rewards those who earnestly seek him.

Hebrews 11:6, NIV

So then *faith* comes by hearing, and *hearing by the word of God.*

Romans 10:17, NKJV

But the man who has doubts is condemned if he eats, because his eating is not from faith; and *everything that does not come from faith is sin.*

Romans 14:23, NIV

Clearly no one is justified before God by the law, because, *"The righteous will live by faith."* The law is not based on faith; on the contrary, "The man who does these things will live by them."

Galatians 3:11-12, NIV

This righteousness from God comes through *faith* in Jesus Christ to all who *believe.*

Romans 3:22, NIV

God presented him as a sacrifice of atonement, through *faith* in his blood. He did this to demonstrate his justice, because in his forbearance he had left the sins committed beforehand unpunished — he did it to demonstrate his justice at the present time, so as to be just and the one who justifies those who have *faith* in Jesus.

Where, then, is boasting? It is excluded. On what principle? On that of observing the law? No, but on that of *faith.* For we maintain that a man is *justified by faith* apart from observing the law.

Romans 3:27-28, NIV

Therefore, since we have been *justified through faith*, we have peace with God through our Lord Jesus Christ, through whom we have *gained access by faith* into this grace in which we now stand.

Romans 5:1-2, NIV

For it is by grace you have been saved, *through faith* — and this not from yourselves, it is the gift of God — not by works, so that no one can boast.

Ephesians 2:8-9, NIV

Christ redeemed us from the curse of the law by becoming a curse for us, for it is written: "Cursed is everyone who is hung on a tree." He redeemed us in order that the blessing given to Abraham might come to the Gentiles through Christ Jesus, so that *by faith we might receive the promise of the Spirit.*

Galatians 3:13-14, NIV

Let us draw near to God with a sincere heart in full assurance of *faith....*

Hebrews 10:22, NIV

In him and *through faith in him* we may approach God with freedom and confidence.

Ephesians 3:12, NIV

"Have faith in God," Jesus answered. "I tell you the truth, if anyone says to this mountain, 'Go, throw yourself into the sea,' and *does not doubt* in his heart but *believes* that what he says will happen, it will be done for him. Therefore I tell you, whatever you ask for in prayer, believe that you have received it, and it will be yours."

Mark 11:22-24, NIV

It is written: "I *believed*; therefore I have spoken." With that same spirit of *faith* we also *believe* and therefore speak....

2 Corinthians 4:13, NIV

"I tell you the truth, if you have *faith* as small as a mustard seed, you can say to this mountain, 'Move from here to there' and it will move. Nothing will be impossible for you."

Matthew 17:20, NIV

"Everything is possible for him who *believes*."

Mark 9:23, NIV

"So keep up your courage, men, for I have *faith* in God that it will happen just as he told me."

Acts 27:25, NIV

I have been crucified with Christ; it is no longer I who live, but Christ lives in me; and the life which I now live in the flesh *I live by faith in the Son of God*, who loved me and gave Himself for me.

Galatians 2:20, NKJV

We live *by faith*, not by sight.

2 Corinthians 5:7, NIV

So then, just as you received Christ Jesus as LORD, continue to live in him, rooted and built up in him, strengthened in the *faith* as you were taught, and overflowing with thankfulness.

Colossians 2:6-7, NIV

In addition to all this, take up the shield of *faith*, with which you can extinguish all the flaming arrows of the evil one.

Ephesians 6:16, NIV

Be on your guard; stand firm in the *faith*; be men of courage; be strong.

1 Corinthians 16:13, NIV

Examine yourselves to see whether you are in the *faith*; test yourselves. Do you not realize that Christ Jesus is in you — unless, of course, you fail the test?

2 Corinthians 13:5, NIV

The examination is pretty simple. Look inside and see what you believe. And just to help you out, I'll let you in on a little secret...there isn't a gray area with this thing. It is either black or white, hot or cold. Either you believe God's Word or you don't.

## God's Word Is His Bond
## He Won't Go Against His Word to Meet Your Need

See, there is one thing you've got to understand about God. He is not going to go against His own Word to meet your need. No matter how hard your background was or what dire situations you find yourself in today, you must realize that it is impossible for God to disregard His Word for your sake. If He did, you would be able to rightly call Him prejudiced. And that is one thing you can't do!

God doesn't make exceptions when it comes to His Word. If His Word says that **this righteousness from God comes through faith in Jesus Christ to all who believe,** then it does! If His Word says that **Christ redeemed us from the curse of the law by becoming a curse for us...** then it's true! If His Word says that **everything that does not come from faith is sin,** then it is! If His Word says **and without faith it is impossible to please God...**then that's true too! (Romans 3:22; Galatians 3:13; Romans 14:23; Hebrews 11:6, NIV).

God doesn't back off His Word. He means what He says and He says what He means! So by the same token, if His Word (Ephesians 3:20 again) says that He is **able to do exceeding abundantly above all that we ask or think, according to the power that worketh in us,** then it is true. He meant it. And regardless of your past experiences, you *will not* receive **exceeding abundantly above all that you ask or think** if that power is *not working* in you. The Scripture tells you how it works. It's *your* job to line up with the Scripture and make it work for you!

If you want a manifestation of blessing from the Lord and you just can't seem to receive it, then maybe it's time to re-evaluate your thinking. Do you think that God will bless you no matter what you do? Do you think that He'll cut you some slack because of your past experiences and come through with a manifestation? No matter how much you beat yourself over the head, it won't amount to much if you don't do what God said. His way is simple. It really is. So forget about fighting His ways and start working 'em!

## So What Will You Take?

You know, it sort of relates to what I always say to Christians who are straddling the fence. I say, "Don't go to hell serving Jesus! If you are going to hell, go with gusto! Drink as much booze as you can, run around with as many women as you can find and sin as many different ways as you can think up! Because if you're going to hell, this life holds the only happiness you'll ever see.

But if you want to live for Jesus and one day make heaven your home, then go at it with gusto! Speak the Word! Heal the sick! Raise the dead! Freely give and freely receive!

This same thing applies with believing in The God of Too Much. If you are going to believe that God can save you, then why not believe the rest of the book, too?! Why not believe the whole Bible?! Apply it to your life! Forget about straddling the fence of unbelief! Put aside the way your natural mind thinks for a while and start hearing God with your ears, receiving Him with your mind and believing Him with your heart.

Then, put some action behind your attitude! Stretch your faith and believe God for the miraculous! Remember, God isn't prejudiced. He won't treat anyone else better than you. But He will obey His Word. He will do "exceeding abundantly above all that you ask or think, according to the power that worketh in you." No exceptions. No prejudice. It's all there for you to do the taking. So what will you take? Salvation? Health? Prosperity? Peace in your home? Joy in your heart? What will you open up to God with? What will you allow Him to do exceeding...abundantly...above all?

As for me, I'm not picking and choosing what I'll receive from God. Since God isn't prejudiced and He's offering so much, I'm not wasting time trying to decide what I want most. Whatever the Lord's got for me, I want! And do you know what? Everything I've got, He wants! That's the trade! And man, it's a good one!

# Chapter Thirteen
## God Isn't Looking to Take From You, He's Looking to Give to You!

In my twenty years of ministry, it has never ceased to amaze me how many people refuse to take God up on the trade, even if they know that He can make their lives better.

I believe it's for one reason: fear. They fear that God will "make" them do something they don't want to. Like His sole purpose is to find what will make them squirm the most and then — *zap!* — make them do it! I think everybody ought to take a minute to search their heart and find out if they are harboring a bit of that kind of belief. Ask yourself: am I holding back a part of my life? Am I afraid to give my whole self over to God? If so, why? Do I think that He is out to make my life a living hell? Go ahead. Ask yourself the questions. The answers to those questions will tell you whether you believe God is a good god, or an evil god who's out to getcha!

As for me, I'm not scared that God is going to ask me to do something I don't want to do. And that is no little thing. That is a big thing! Most Christians I meet are scared God is going to "make" them do something or give something they don't want to. So they hold back going the distance for Him. Later, they come begging for His help when it all goes to pot.

Not me! Why? Because I know my God! God is not looking to take *from* His children, He's looking to give *to* His children. Guess what? I'm His kid! I'm an heir through Jesus! He's looking to give to me!

## Oh, No! God's Going to Make Me Give All My Money Away!

Another big thing people I meet fear is this: *if I get close to God I'm afraid He'll make me give all my money away.* Well, let me set your mind at ease a bit: you are not the rich young ruler of Luke 18:18. Jesus did not tell everybody to give away all they had back then, and He isn't doing it much now. I mean, He only told twelve guys to leave their jobs and follow Him. He didn't preach "Give everything you own away" to everybody who came along, He just told it to one man! And many scholars today theorize that Jesus was considering picking the rich young ruler to be one of His twelve disciples, to replace Judas.

So don't sweat it!

Jesus did teach about sowing and reaping, though. Why? Because sowing and reaping is God's law for provision. You can't get around it. Like I said earlier, God instituted sowing and reaping *before* the fall of man. Go ahead, look it up in

Genesis. In fact, seed was the second thing (after dominion) that God gave Adam. Why? For provision! He said, "Adam, plant this! Plant it or you'll starve, boy!"

God talked about it in Genesis. Jesus talked about it in Mark. The Parable of the Sower in Mark 4 is the most important parable Jesus ever taught, and it dealt with sowing and reaping. How can I make such a big claim? Because I'm quoting Jesus. **Know ye not this parable? and how then will ye know all parables?** (Mark 4:13). In other words, "Hey, if you don't understand this, you won't understand anything!" So, obviously, it has to be the most important one.

Now, I know that some people think He wasn't talking about prosperity. I am of the opinion that Jesus was talking about *everything* in life, *including* prosperity. Come on, though! Even if you think He was talking only about the spiritual realm, you have to notice that the symbol he used to get His point across was crops! God was talking to Adam about crops in Genesis. Jesus was talking to us about crops in Mark. And what does a crop symbolize? Food! Provision!

If you plant one acre of corn, can you eat the one-hundred-fold return on that one acre? Can you and your family digest 100 acres of corn? Give me a break! You eat what you can, then you sell the rest and make a profit. That's provision! It's God's plan to bless you so that you in turn can be a blessing to the families of the earth! (Genesis 12:3.) But how can you bless the families of the earth if you aren't blessed? Of course, if I started teaching all that I know about sowing and reaping, it would fill another book! So I won't go into much more detail. But I do believe God has given me a revelation on the financial end of prosperity, and, if He allows me, I hope to publish a book on the subject in more detail soon.

The most important thing that I want to share with you concerning this subject is this: *Jesus spent most of His time in the Parable of the Sower warning against sowing unwisely.* He told how a harvest on the seed could be different depending on how and where the seed is sown. That is important information. It can literally make or break you.

You should study the Parable of the Sower. Pray about it. Like Jesus said, if you don't understand this parable, how will you know any parable? This is crucial in all aspects of life, including giving and receiving. If you apply it to your financial situation, Jesus' teaching will show you that you just can't throw seed; you have to sow seed. Scattering seed is foolish. Planting it in good soil and tending to it until it produces fruit is wise.

Another Scripture that is crucial in understanding giving is 2 Corinthians 9:7. The end of this Scripture warns you not to give out of necessity but to purpose in your heart what you will give and to do it cheerfully.

Purpose in your heart *before* you give. That way, your emotions won't rule your giving. You won't be *need* motivated, you'll be *seed* motivated. Sometimes a need can make you feel guilty and you dig deeper into your wallet than you originally purposed in your heart. This can be good if the Lord is leading you, but check to see that it's not your own emotions ruling you. God never told you to give with your emotions. He never told you to give out of love.

Yeah, believe it or not, it's true. Look it up. He told you to *live in love, give in faith!* So don't give unwisely. Faith brings a harvest back to you. Love doesn't. Sow wisely! Recognize what you are giving and believe in faith for a return. That harvest is rightfully yours. Don't neglect tending to that seed sown by just throwing something in the offering plate and forgetting about it. Tend to it with an expectancy (hope) and belief (faith) that a harvest will come up on that seed. Faith will make it grow and in due season you shall reap the thirty-, sixty- or hundred-fold return!

## Guilt-Giving Isn't From God!

God isn't going to make you give to every ministry that comes along. Hey, let me tell you, I don't! And I don't feel guilty about it. I'm free from that junk! There are thousands, probably millions, of great organizations that are doing wonderful things in the earth. But God hasn't called me to be a partner with every one of them. He's called me to be a covenant partner with certain ones. The important part is that I obey His voice, not the voice of emotionalism. Sure, there are many doing good. But I give where God tells me to give.

You can't get under the pressure of giving to every organization. Don't let some preacher on television who is begging for a pledge cause you to give out of emotionalism. He may be in need of the money, sure. But do you know what? He might not be good soil. And God might not have ever told him to go on television. So pray about it. If God impresses upon your heart to become his partner, then do it. If He doesn't, then don't! Don't just get your checkbook out because somebody's crying on the tube. First, think about what they are saying. If they just told you that God can do anything and yet they're begging you for money to stay on the air, what they're really saying is this: "God can do everything but pay my bills." Hint,

hint...it's probably poor soil. You won't get a good harvest planting in that kind of soil. Read the Parable of the Sower again in Mark 4.

It's not your job to become a partner with every ministry that visits your church, is on television or sends you mail. So don't get under condemnation about it. God won't ask you for what you haven't got. He'll provide seed for the sower.

And don't worry, God won't tell you to reach for the largest bill in your wallet. Your preacher might, but God won't! That isn't even scriptural so don't let anybody fool you. Remember, while God picks the multiplication (thirty-, sixty- or one-hundred-fold), you pick the denomination ($5, $20, $100 and so on). Be wise and you will prosper!

## Give Where God Tells You To

You must give where God tells you to. Of course, give your tithe (which is the Lord's according to Malachi 3:10) where you're fed regularly. You wouldn't eat at McDonald's and pay at Burger King. Don't go to church and eat a good spiritual meal there and give your tithe to another church! Give where you're fed. Or, like one minister I know says, "Dance with the one who brought you." This is just honorable. If somebody blesses you, enriches your life, then they ought to be blessed.

But above the tithe, give offerings when and where God impresses you to give them. God will cause you to prayerfully and financially covenant with a ministry; He may ask you to covenant with several. Of that you can be certain. It's His will that the whole earth learn about Jesus. Obey His voice and give to the ministry or ministries He puts on your heart.

Become a regular prayer and financial partner with only those who God impresses you to partner with. That way, you'll know you're giving into good soil that will yield a harvest.

God takes care of His people. He pours out blessing on those ministries which He's called. He will cause different men and women on the earth to covenant with different ministries on the earth so that they all grow to the stature that He intended.

I believe that if everybody prayed — truly prayed and sought the Lord — before they gave, we would weed out the religious crooks and uplift the men and women who are truly called by God to preach this Gospel to the world.

## He Provides Seed to the Sower

If God wants you to pour out a part of your life or provision into someone else's life, He will provide whatever it is He wants you to pass along. God provides seed to the sower. (2 Corinthians 9:10.)

When God tells me to give something, I don't refuse Him. Why? Because I know God! I don't just know about Him, I know Him! It isn't going to hurt me. I might have to step out in faith, but I won't have to sweat and cry over loss. God won't stand for that! He will not only provide seed to the sower, He's going to repay me way more than what I put out! God is faithful. He won't be a debtor. I know the laws of sowing and reaping. I know that it isn't in God's nature to allow lack. You may allow lack through ignorance or refusal to obey His laws, but God never will. It is His will that you are blessed, whole and full of joy! **Beloved, I wish above all things that thou mayest**

**prosper and be in health, even as thy soul prospereth** (3 John 1:2). Since all Scripture is divine revelation from God, I take that Scripture to heart! It's God's will that you lack no good thing. (Psalm 84:11.)

God wants you to have too much in every area of your life. So, don't hold back with Him! He's only got good things for you. Don't worry, He isn't out to getcha! He's out to give to you!

*God is good!* If you have a hard time with prosperity, say this to yourself out loud every time you start to feel guilt rise up. Retrain your mind to believe that God is good. What He has done for others, He will do for you. As long as you put Him first and obey His Word, God is "able to do exceeding abundantly above all that you can ask or think according to the power that worketh in you!" This is His Word. He makes no exceptions to His Word. And He shows no prejudice to His people.

## Somebody's in the Woodpile!

Since we're talking about prejudice, I thought I'd share a funny little story with you. A while back a man approached me with a strange question. He'd heard me make references to my heritage before and so he approached me with a curious look on his face and began to ask a few questions.

"You're a Cajun man, aren't you?" he asked.

"Yes, sir," I smiled back.

"Well, shouldn't Cajuns be kind of dark-skinned and brown-eyed? You're light-skinned and blue-eyed."

*Hmmm. That's a good question*, I thought. I laughed to myself and then I answered it the best I could.

"Well, there's somebody in the woodpile. And we don't know who it is and we didn't ask!"

"Well, who did your ancestors marry?" he asked with curiosity.

"Anybody they could find!"

When you live on the swamp all your life and the only things you see are alligators, any woman will look good! So when some toothless woman comes along and you go, "Mama! What's happening! You lookin' *fine!*" That woman will put a kiss on you so sloppy it'll cover you whole face!

I don't know who everybody married back then! Obviously they weren't too prejudiced though, because just take a look at me! My hair is grey/white now but it used to be chocolate brown. I loved it. It was beautiful! But get this: I grow a red beard but all the hair on the rest of my body is blond! Figure that one out! There is no telling who's in the woodpile in my family!

I've had people ask me, "What is a Cajun?"

By now, who knows? I do know that originally Cajuns were called Acadians and they were people who emigrated from France (because they got kicked out) and went to Nova Scotia. Then (because they got kicked out again) they traveled to America and followed the Mississippi River to the very end of Louisiana, where the river empties into the Gulf of Mexico. Most settled along the waterways (bayous) that wind through the land where the swamp waters were plentiful with seafood and the land was full of wild deer and duck. (Sounds like a brochure, huh?)

Cajun isn't a race of people really...I think it's more like a culture. Although the Cajun people are still predominantly French, we've got healthy mixtures of people from places like Germany and Ireland. And of course there were many Native Americans here, so they're in the woodpile, too.

To be honest, by the time you get this far South, just about every one is mixed and few are pure-blood anything. You know us French...we're a lovin' people! Whoever came to town was good enough to marry!

Cajuns are just part of the melting pot of America. But in this melting pot, we cook better food than anywhere you'll ever go! You get all of those different people swapping recipes and spices and you've got one good gumbo! Some people think Cajun food is just hot, but those of us who live here know better. Most people outside of south Louisiana think a bottle of cayenne pepper is all you need to make food "Cajun." But it's the flavor, not the fire, that makes a Crawfish Bisque so good you want to slap your grandma!

But you know, God isn't prejudiced like people are. He doesn't care if you're a pure-bred proper Englishman or a mixed-breed casual Cajun. God loves our differences and treats all of His children as if we were His favorite. Why? Because He can't help Himself! His love is too consuming! It's His nature to pour out too much of it!

God is looking for a people who He can intimately talk with on a daily basis. People who are unafraid of Him and who are ready to accept the love that He's pouring out. God is looking for people who are willing to put aside the world's views and start paying attention to His views. Simply...to drop the religion and begin having a relationship with Him.

## Chapter Fourteen
# Humility: It Isn't What You Think It Is

For years Satan has tried to cloak poverty in humility. He's basically tried to make it religious so nobody would question it. Many think that poverty makes you humble. And in one sense, it does. But it isn't the humbleness God spoke about. It's the warped view of humbleness most people have today. Say the word "humble" today and most people will think of a man with his head lowered, eyes to the floor, nervous and fragile, with very little to say except self-abasing remarks about himself. Basically, most think of someone who has no self-esteem and thinks very little of himself.

This is not God's view of humility. It is a false humility and was not at all what God intended for man to be. In the Bible, humility is a word that is often paired with other words like patience and righteousness, grace and gentleness. You will find it right alongside other words like wisdom, honor and even salvation.

Humility can be a powerful asset to a Christian's life. Satan knows this and that is why he has tried to virtually destroy real humility by linking it with self-abasing and esteem-destroying poverty.

In fact, in 1 Peter 5:5, the Scripture tells us to **be clothed with humility**. In other words, to cover your flesh with it! If you're practicing humility your flesh really won't be able to show off. Why? Because it'll be covered up.

See, true humility isn't self-abasing. When practicing humility you shouldn't feel like a low-down dirty piece of trash. You shouldn't be acting like a stepping stone or a whipping boy. That's warped. God created you to be majestic! His redeemed child! Righteous! Worthy of a crown! You're awesome to God. He sent His Son Jesus to die for you. Do you think He'd do that if He thought you were nothing but a piece of trash? You're something, all right! You are filled with "too much" of someone great: Jesus!

## Through Jesus' Blood We're Made Righteous!

When Adam sinned against God, mankind flew into a tailspin. Since then, we've all inherited the sin nature, a destructive nature that is prideful, competitive and filled with angst and fury. The sin nature is rooted in confusion. It causes some to strive for superiority. It causes others to spiral down in despair. We can't become righteous *on our own* with that kind of nature stuck in us. We can't come back into right standing with God on *our own* when that kind of nature is dwelling in our hearts. We're unworthy *on our own*. That's why God sent Jesus to the earth: so we wouldn't have to be like those living in Old Testament times. We got more than a slain lamb. We got The Lamb Slain Before the Foundation of the World! Jesus, God's Only Begotten Son!

Through Jesus' blood we are made righteous, worthy, able to receive **exceeding abundantly above all that we ask or think, according to the power that worketh in us!** Glory to Jesus! His blood did it! We couldn't do it on our own! We had to have His sacrifice to wash away our sin so that we could once again communicate with the Almighty God!

So, where does the world's view of humility fit in there? It doesn't. It doesn't have a place at all. God's true humility, on the other hand, does have a place.

God's true humility raises you to your rightful position in Jesus. It gives you complete peace knowing that you have been made righteous — knowing that the slate has been wiped clean — and you are now able to begin again. A new life in Christ Jesus! Glory!

## True Humility Isn't Competitive or Superior; It Recognizes Equality

When you walk in true humility, you recognize your place in Christ Jesus. You recognize His goodness and mercy. And you live your life with a thankful heart. Now here is where you're walking in real humility: you recognize where you have come from (sin), what Jesus has done for you (washed sin away and brought you into right standing with God), and what you're doing now (being thankful, telling others and walking in His commandments). Humility is being aware of *who you are* and being aware of *who others are* in God's sight.

There is nothing self-destructive about God's humility. It doesn't ruin your self-esteem, it betters your self-esteem. How? It does it by taking out the competitiveness between men, by taking man out of the race for superiority and bringing him into equality through redemption. This is true humility. And if we could all learn to walk in just a fraction of it, we'd see many of the dilemmas of mankind brought to a halt. You see, racism can't remain in a person who is humble. Pride can't remain in a person who is humble. Humility could wipe out the stressful, striving nature of man quick!

Humility is from God. It is uplifting, not destructive, to the heart of man. And the only way to experience this true humility is through fellowship with Jesus. Time with Jesus is the key to remaining humble. You can't be haughty in the presence of the Creator of the universe. Prayer will put that in check quick!

## True Humility Causes You to Prefer One Another

There is peace in being thankful to your Creator for giving you a new life! There is peace in knowing that no one on earth was created like you and no one on earth can do what you can do. This shouldn't make you haughty; it should make you humble! Why? Because it means that you are singular, individual and unique to God. And there is no one on this earth that is greater or lesser than you. There is no one to compete with for superiority.

We all were created and re-created by God. We are all different and yet the same; individual and yet part of an elite group. We're beings made in the image of the Almighty God! Amazing, huh?

And what better way to show that we are God's own than to prefer one another? To give credit to one another for accomplishments? To give honor to one another for simply being a child of God? To compliment each other and praise God for each other's gifts, talents and altogether unique personalities? What better way to show our humility and love to God by showing His children generosity, kindness and joyful love!

This is God's humility. Do you get the picture? Humility like this flows from His heart to our heart through prayer and fellowship with Him. We can't get it on our own. We get it from Jesus, from time spent with Him, from recognizing His goodness as being overwhelmingly too much!

Humility mixed with love: it is essential to our well-being, our sense of security and our peace of mind that we understand what true humility is and do our best to show it to others.

## Leave Your False Humility at the Foot of the Cross

Peace. Everybody wants it. And that's where Jesus comes in. There is peace in knowing who you are in Jesus. It sets your soul at ease to know that **God so loved the world that He gave His only begotten Son, that whoever believes in Him should not perish but have everlasting life** (John 3:16, NKJV).

To know that you are righteous, saved by grace through Jesus' precious blood, humbles you. You can't help but have a thankful heartwhen you realize just what Jesus did on that cross. It'll humble you quick! It'll make you cry out, "Thank you, Jesus!" A brutal, cruel death...just for you.

That is why it is so aggravating to me to see Satan warp humility and cause men to forsake the promises Jesus died to give, calling themselves unworthy to receive the blessings. And then living downtrodden lives because of it.

How arrogant! What a spectacle of false humility to not even take what Jesus died so horribly to give! To leave the promise of health at the cross. To leave the promise of provision at the cross. To leave the promise of joy at the cross. To leave all that Jesus' death bought at the foot of that bloody cross.

Is that humility? Is it true humility to reject all that His death bought? If it is, I'd forsake that humility! Out of compassion for Jesus, I'd forsake it! Out of honor for what He has done for me, I'd forsake that kind of humility. Wouldn't you?

But thank God we don't have to forsake anything good. No. Because leaving just one promise at the foot of the cross in the name of humility should open your eyes to the Truth. It should reveal, expose, bring into the light the lie that Satan has sold the church for centuries. Unworthiness is not humility. He has preached that far too long. And it is time that we open our eyes and do our best to expose what can only be called false humility! It is not from God. That "I'm not worthy" mentality rips at the very fabric of redemption. And I'll have no part in that whatsoever.

## Insecurity in the Body of Christ Is a Terminator: It Seeks and Destroys the Brotherhood of Men

This isn't some theology. This isn't something that you can't do. It takes effort. And it will take honesty. But more than that, it will take prayer. Because before you can walk in true humility, you have to really know who you are in Jesus. You have to be secure. And let me tell you, insecurity is straight from the pit. It breeds false humility. It is what causes people to act haughty. It is what causes them to be jealous of other people's accomplishments. Insecurity is what causes ridges between people. It is a Terminator, seeking to destroy the brotherhood of men. Insecurity eats away at a person's self-worth, at their position in Jesus. It causes a person to look at another with envy and greed.

How do you know if you have it? For one thing, look for pride. Let's say you work in the same field as your friend and he just got promoted. He comes to you full of joy with a big smile on his face. You're his friend. You're the first one he wants to tell.

Now, you already know he got the promotion. You heard it through the grapevine. But what do you feel like inside? Are you so thrilled that you run up to him in joy, slap him on the back and congratulate him for the promotion? Do you offer to help him in the transition time? Tell him that you've been praying for him? Continually congratulate him for his talents and hard work?

Or, do you feel a hesitancy in your heart and reply, "Oh, I heard. Congratulations." Do you have a hard time congratulating him? Do you feel true excitement for him? Is it hard to say good things? Do you struggle with it a little? I'll take it further. Can you be just as happy for him as you would have been if you had gotten the promotion?

Insecurity makes a person uncomfortable with others' accomplishments. They aren't secure in themselves and, even though they might not think so, they're still living in fierce competition with others. Other people's talents make them uneasy. Other people's gifts make them uneasy. If people pay too much attention to someone other than themselves, they feel uneasy. If any of this sounds familiar, if any of it hits a nerve with you, then congratulations...you're being honest! And, man, is that hard to come by these days!

## Honesty: the First Step to Maturity

I believe that it takes a level of maturity in Jesus to really walk in humility, to shed the tight scaly skin of insecurity. A mature person in Jesus isn't afraid of others' accomplishments. He doesn't feel less of a person when his brother or sister in Christ succeeds. His self-worth isn't dependent on those around him. His self-worth is dependent on Jesus, on his view of himself as a child of the living God.

That kind of maturity takes real honesty. It takes noticing when that uneasy feeling creeps up in your heart and tries to plant envy. It takes awareness of what you feel in your own heart and what is coming out of your own mouth. If your mouth is a garbage can and you say more trash than good things, then you could safely say that trash is in your heart. The root is probably insecurity. You need to know in your heart, and not just your mind, who you've become through Jesus. You need maturity.

Maturity comes from spending time with the One Who searches out the hidden things in your heart. You don't have to spend hours every morning in prayer to become a mature, holy, humble child of God. You just need to exercise honesty and openness in prayer and effort in life. If you're honest with God, you'll be open to hear His voice. And He will tell you where you went wrong. His Holy Spirit will warn you when false humility and/or envy creeps up on you.

Then you have to exercise effort and self-control. You immediately cast envy and jealously down. You immediately clothe yourself in humility. True humility. The kind that imparts life and a strong sense of peace and security to you. Why fret over someone else's accomplishment? Why allow Satan to steal joy from another child of God? Protect that joy! Combat that sin nature with thoughts of love. If insecurity is in your heart, then dig out its root. Dig out that seed of envy by praying. Jerk that thick, slimy root out of your heart by speaking out loud to the Lord and honestly laying your heart's feelings on the table. Be honest. See what's in there. (You might be surprised to hear how much crud comes out of your heart. Selfish, competitive roots of bitterness are famous for hiding all sorts of trash.) Then ask for forgiveness. Be repentant. Remember Psalm 51:10, which says, **Create in me a clean heart, O God; and renew a right spirit within me**. Speak to the Lord and allow His love to cleanse you, to renew a right spirit within you.

Honest prayer like this will create a humble spirit within you. You'll be able to feel what it is like to be humble. You'll be able to feel self-worth through Jesus and to exercise humility by turning the tables on jealousy and thinking good about someone else. Deliberately think of the other person and speak good things about them.

Next time you see that brother or sister, go out of your way to be sincere and share in the joy they feel in their accomplishment. Lavish compliments and praise on them. They are unique individuals with special talents, so show joy and sincere excitement for what is going on in their lives.

If it's difficult at first, don't get discouraged. Keep them in your prayers and continue to exercise humility. Sow it.

Sow it bountifully in the lives of others. Sow humility. Sow love. Sow joy. Sow honor. God will, in no small way, repay you.

## Chapter Fifteen
# All He Needs Is a Connection

Some people don't believe this. They believe that God is able to do exceeding abundantly above all that we ask or think...but they don't believe the end of the Scripture that says according to the power that worketh in us. That's the most important part! That is the valve God put into place concerning this Scripture. We squeeze off the amount we have faith to believe for. Some people let out just a trickle of God is able to do exceeding abundantly above all that we ask or think.... Others let out a steady stream. And some are doing their best to hold on while the power is gushing from their valve! According to the power that worketh in us is the valve that releases God is able to do exceeding abundantly above all that we ask or think! It's what makes it happen!

People who don't believe that are usually the people who are always struggling with something. They either don't believe they have any responsibility in the matter or they'd rather keep the problem than fight the good fight of faith.

They're waiting on God to drop money in their laps. They're waiting on God to heal their broken and bruised bodies. They're waiting on God to change their circumstances. They're waiting and waiting and waiting.

But let me tell you something: we have to take responsibility for ourselves...for our own faith. No one can do it for us. We have to believe God. Not just with lip service, but with heart service.

Jesus has finished His work. He was pure. He was innocent. And He died a horrible death on the cross so that you could open that valve and receive too much of God's goodness. Belief in Him is the valve that allows us to receive a free-flowing river of salvation, healing, prosperity, joy and all the other "too much" promises flowing from the Throne of Grace.

## *Wham!* And You're Hit!

The electricity is in the air. The power is in the air. All God needs is a connection, a spark, an avenue in which to unfurl His power.

Ben Franklin proved that when he flew that kite up there with a key on it. God had power literally in the sky. A storm came and *wham!* It hit that key and lit up Ben's hair like Bozo the Clown! Electricity! It was there all the time. Ben just found the connection. And later we figured out how to harness it and use it to man's benefit. But do you know that even today man has not figured out how to store energy? We can use electricity. But nobody's figured out how to store a lightning bolt! God knows how. He is limitless. In Him are secrets that seem unfathomable to man's mind.

The power of God is like electricity. You're like the valve, the connection. He flows through you. Get that attitude of faith in check. Be obedient and let Him go! Don't stand back and wait for lightning to strike. Be the receptacle. Get yourself as close to the power as you can. Be that key floating in the midst of a stormy sky...ready, willing and able to harness the power from on high! You do your part, the possible. God will strike down with the impossible! *Wham!* New ideas for your business! *Wham!* Prophetic utterances for those in need! *Wham!* Supernatural healing in your body! *Wham!* Peace that passes all understanding while you're in the darkest hour! *Wham!* Financial increase just when you needed it! *Wham!* *Wham! Wham!* The power of God striking your life and setting you ablaze! That is God's way. And it isn't enough. It's too much!

## Keep the Faith Until You Hear *Well Done!*

God wants to give you eternal life after you die. And He wants to give you sufficiency for all things while you're here on the earth.

God wants to meet your need according to *His* riches in glory. You know, people have been using their faith in conjunction with that Scripture in Philippians for almost two thousand years. And it hasn't exhausted God's account yet! That's how much "too much" The God of Too Much has got!

God wants to give you all the promises in the Book. He "wishes above all things that you prosper and be in health, even as your soul prospers." (3 John 2, author's paraphrase.) But receiving God's promises is all up to you.

It's up to you whether you will *believe God* instead of *believe in* God...*know God* instead of *know about God*. Ultimately, it's up to you whether or not you allow God to do "exceeding abundantly above all that you ask or think *according to the power that worketh in you*."

Before I leave you to contemplate all you've read so far, I want to remind you: never limit your asking or thinking. You can't exhaust God's resources, even if you try. He really is *too much*.

And there is nothing good in this life that you cannot have or do when you rely upon Him. When you begin walking in the principles I've written in this book, I must warn you that there may be people who will really disagree with you. There might be those who will tell you that faith isn't true. And if you believe them, you can keep on living with problems for the rest of your days. I don't know about you, but I need answers! And faith in God is *the* answer.

When you hear someone tell you to put a limit on what you ask God, don't sweat it. Just remember this: that person probably got out of balance in his life and let the Devil rob him. Maybe God blessed, and, instead of blessing others, he got in the flesh with it. So maybe he just wants to make sure that you don't get in the flesh with your prosperity. But you haven't ever gotten out of balance! And if you keep your eyes on Jesus, you never will.

So don't worry about what people say. Let negative words roll off you like water off a duck's back. Fight the good fight. Finish your course. Keep the faith. When it's all said and done you'll stand before The God of Too Much with a lifetime of adventures in faith behind you. Pleased and proud, your Heavenly Father will one day look you right in the eye and say, **Well done, thou good and faithful servant...enter thou into the joy of thy lord** (Matthew 25:21)!

# Do You Know God?

Or do you just know *about* God? Is Jesus part of your life? Is He your friend? Can you talk to Him? If you've answered "no" to any of these questions then I'd like to take the opportunity to introduce you to the best friend you'll ever have: Jesus!

Jesus isn't a fairy tale. He is real. He is personal. And He's ready to come into your life and help you make a change if you want Him to.

Whether you've never asked Him to come into your life or you are simply not living how you should be, would you pray this prayer with me?

*"Lord Jesus, I ask you to forgive me of all my sins. I confess that I am a sinner before You this day. I denounce Satan and all his works. I ask you to come into my heart and change me. Right now, Jesus, I want you to know that I believe with all my heart that you are the Son of God, that you died on the cross for the sins of the world and that you rose from the dead. I confess these things with my mouth, so all of heaven and earth can hear it. I'm saved!*

*Jesus, reveal yourself to me. Reveal your nature to me. I want to experience "too much" in my spiritual life, my physical life and my financial life. I promise that I will not consume your precious abundance solely upon myself, but I will establish your covenant upon this earth. From this day forward I will tell others about you. I will walk in faith. I will excel in all that I put my hand to do because I will be doing your will, Jesus. You will be my guide and my best friend. Today...I begin again. I am a new creature in You, Christ Jesus! Everywhere I go, I will let Your light shine through me.*

*I pray this prayer to the Father, in the name of Jesus. Amen!"*

Haaahh! You made it! You've just been born again! (John 3:3.) Shout! Your name is now written in the Lamb's Book of Life. Heaven will be your home when you die and adventures await you from this moment on! Would you do me a favor? Write me and tell me if you prayed this prayer. Let me know that you've made Jesus your Lord!

I may never get to meet you face to face in this life. But in heaven, who knows? I might live right next door to you! If I do, I'll be at your house every day! I'll slide over on the gold streets in my socks and stick my head through your window! We'll have a great time. Until then, may The God of Too Much bless you in everything you set your hand to do!


Much Love and Blessings,


Jesse Duplantis

# About the Author

Jesse Duplantis is a dynamic evangelist called to minister God's message of salvation through Jesus Christ to the world. From New Orleans, Louisiana, Jesse is anointed by God with a unique preaching ministry that melts even the hardest heart with hilarious illustrations and strong biblical preaching.

Having been in full-time evangelistic ministry since 1978, Jesse's primary goal is to spread the Gospel. He has become a popular guest speaker at church meetings, conventions, seminars, Bible colleges and Christian television programs across America. His anointed sermons point sinners to Calvary and motivate Christians to exercise their authority over the devil by realizing their position in Christ.

Jesse believes that Christianity is not just something you talk about on Sunday, it is a day-to-day fellowship with the Lord Jesus. It is this close fellowship with Jesus that makes the impossible suddenly possible.

Today, Jesse's entire life is devoted to reaching the lost as well as strengthening the Christian in their daily walk with Christ. Jesse's weekly thirty-minute television program has touched millions of lives through secular and Christian television with the Gospel of Jesus. His program can be seen weekly on Trinity Broadcasting Network and other stations worldwide.

Through anointed biblical preaching, Jesse is bringing God's message of hope to our generation. A message that cuts through all denominational barriers, transcends human hypocrisy and frailty, and reaches the heart of mankind.

To contact the author, write:

Jesse Duplantis

P.O. Box 20149 • New Orleans, Louisiana 70141

Additional copies of this book and Jesse Duplantis'
book, *Heaven — Close Encounters of the God Kind*,
are available from your local bookstore.

## The Harrison House Vision

Proclaiming the truth and power
Of the Gospel of Jesus Christ
With excellence;

Challenging Christians to
Live victoriously,
Grow spiritually,
Know God intimately.